ISBN 13: 978-0-9847976-0-8

Library of Congress Control Number: 2011961909

    Dwivedi, Rajiv.
    How To Compete With The Industry Giants: The field manual to an entrepreneurial society / Rajiv Dwivedi.
           ISBN 978-0-9847976-0-8

The paper used in this publication meets the minimum requirements of the American National Standard for Information Sciences – Permanence of Paper for Printed Library Materials, ANSI Z39.48-1992.

To my wife Christy, kids Alex and Rachel, Dad, The Gartners, The Dwivedis and in memory of my mother, Urmila Dwivedi

"War is just a racket. A racket is best described, I believe, as something that is not what it seems to the majority of people. Only a small inside group knows what it is about. It is conducted for the benefit of the very few at the expense of the masses...

I wouldn't go to war again as I have done to protect some lousy investment of the bankers. There are only two things we should fight for. One is the defense of our homes and the other is the Bill of Rights. War for any other reason is simply a racket.

It may seem odd for me, a military man to adopt such a comparison. Truthfulness compels me to. I spent thirty- three years and four months in active military service as a member of this country's most agile military force, the Marine Corps. I served in all commissioned ranks from Second Lieutenant to Major-General. And during that period, I spent most of my time being a high class muscle- man for Big Business, for Wall Street and for the Bankers. In short, I was a racketeer, a gangster for capitalism.

I suspected I was just part of a racket at the time. Now I am sure of it. Like all the members of the military profession, I never had a thought of my own until I left the service. My mental faculties remained in suspended animation while I obeyed the orders of higher-ups. This is typical with everyone in the military service.

I helped make Mexico, especially Tampico, safe for American oil interests in 1914. I helped make Haiti and Cuba a decent place for the National City Bank boys to collect revenues in. I helped in the raping of half a dozen Central American republics for the benefits of Wall Street. The record of racketeering is long. I helped purify Nicaragua for the international banking house of Brown Brothers in 1909-1912. I brought light to the Dominican Republic for American sugar interests in 1916. In China I helped to see to it that Standard Oil went its way unmolested.

During those years, I had, as the boys in the back room would say, a swell racket. Looking back on it, I feel that I could have given Al Capone a few hints. The best he could do was to operate his racket in three districts. I operated on three continents."

-   Major General Smedley D. Butler, USMC, excerpt
    from 1933 speech

How To Compete With The Industry Giants:

Contents

Introduction

It seems that people have lost the confidence they once took for granted. There is uncertainty about the future valuation of their retirement accounts, their job in a company, the stability of whether their customers can obtain funds to continue to operate and pay on time and in turn if they will be able to stay in business for a long term career. It also seems that there is an opportunity to address this fear head on and know what it takes to compete and make the leap of faith that we can compete as individual contributors, get the funding we need to thrive in our particular fields of expertise, secure loyal customers by adding innovative value that is unique to ourselves, building deep and trusting relationships with everyone around us and restoring the confidence that seems to be lost or eluding people dealing with large enterprises and government.

The common saying that necessity is the mother of invention could be appropriate to the millions of people looking for work wondering what they can do to make ends meet while they are looking for permanent employment in meaningful and fulfilling careers. This book serves as a field manual to help individuals understand what it will take to compete with the industry giants as much as it is a wake-up call to those companies and individuals in large companies who have taken unfair and anti-competitive advantage over individuals. This book is appropriate for anyone currently out of work and actively looking for work, anyone uncertain about the security of his or her future in their current job or anyone under-employed considering the leap into entrepreneurial independence. There are many anecdotal observations that I have drawn from the material I have learned formally, informally and my professional work experiences in various industries over 20 years observing hundreds of successful small, medium and large enterprises and having found my niche among them. Many great organizations have found their niche and built loyal customer relationships through trust over many years of sticking with something and staying true to their beliefs and core values.

My work included with large companies Circuit City Stores, Inc., De La Rue PLC, Kinko's, Inc., my own companies, Carteret Mortgage Corp, and Staples, Inc. as well as serving as a commissioned officer with the US Marines. My work experience in companies allowed me to work with over two hundred employees and interacting with hundreds of business enterprises that were small, medium and large as a negotiator, supplier and customer for the companies that I worked for in various executive capacities. My work experience gave me a unique perspective into small businesses and individual proprietors competing in the open market against larger competitors bent on crushing competition. I am proof positive that anyone can thrive in a career transition from government or military employee to corporate employee to independent operator and receive an abundance of happiness, joy and fulfillment that comes from working for yourself and having a supportive and loving home environment. I am one of the luckiest individuals blessed to be able to put this work together. I have two great kids, a loving and incredibly supportive wife and an incredible extended family that have helped me with every step I have ever taken through life.

This book should give you something to think about if you are considering getting out of a corporate or government job and going out there on your own with special emphasis on the essentials that are necessary to succeed in business. At the fundamental level of starting any business is that you have the family support behind you in knowing what you want to do and are going to do. I would tell anyone that if you can't gain that support and commitment from family then you should rethink going out on your own because it is a commitment to a life beyond 9 to 5 working hours and could lead to strained personal relationships. If you decide that you are going out on your own, this book should serve you well as the field manual on solution selling, leadership traits that are needed to be developed and priority setting to turn innovation ideas into action.

If you have feedback to this book, I would love to hear it. Please share it with me at rajdwivedi@printondemand.net.

Leadership

There is so much information available on the topic of leadership, that one can actually obtain a graduate degree specializing in the study of leadership for the purpose of business management, military scholarship, or biographical scholarship. My effort here in this book is to provide some personal guidance and perspective for you on the level of leadership needed to compete against the best organizations in the world and show where I drew lessons in leadership through anecdotes and reference material included. I aim to provide a working guide as to what traits anyone can develop, recruit and allow to flourish in your personal life, family life or overall organization.

My first introduction to the formal study of leadership came through the US Marines of what they considered the 14 essential traits that leaders of Marines had to possess and master. These leadership traits were the foundation of traits of men and the Marines took it so far as to develop an evaluative performance management system of fitness reports for commissioned officers and non-commissioned officers that graded individuals on these very traits of leadership.

The 14 traits were memorized by all Marines under the acronym JJDIDTIEBUCKLE representing the first letter of each trait below in alphabetical order. I memorized them during boot camp at Parris Island, SC in alphabetical order just to ensure I had mastered all of them. I would always mentally check my alphabetical memorization against the acronym to make sure I didn't miss any of them.

Bearing	Integrity
Courage	Judgment
Decisiveness	Justice
Dependability	Knowledge
Endurance	Loyalty
Enthusiasm	Tact
Initiative	Unselfishness

In applying the 14 traits to practical leadership and management I put my own personal definition to each leadership trait for discussion as the common thread that runs throughout this guide to help any smaller company or individual compete against a larger company. I have also included the US Marine Corps definitions of these traits taken directly from the Marine Corps Leadership handbook and is well known public information for perspective to compare with my personal application of each trait. I think every Marine Commissioned Officer you meet may have their own personal definition and may put special emphasis on a few of these traits that they have valued and can cite as being the core trait to their personal success.

Bearing

Bearing to me meant to keep one's composure and appearance of a stoic, professional indifference to the situation at hand, and giving the appearance at all times to followers who could observe me the appearance of a level head under times of high stress, personal pain or emotionally charged circumstance, and to fight instinctual urges of fight or flight reflex that would have almost any other human being explode in a rage, break down into an emotional fit of sorrow, or otherwise visual complaining, whining and/or moaning about the situation being faced. The military definition of bearing was to maintain the calm demeanor under fire, and the best example I always referred to when understanding this trait of Bearing was the military anecdote from a surviving German soldier telling the story of his unit commander, a captain, occupying a farmhouse on a front line which was a large open field where the lines were drawn between Allied and German infantry forces. The Allied artillery units knew that the German unit's command was set up in the farm house and were adjusting fire on the house, bracketing back and forth until they got closer to the house. The German infantry soldiers were terrified as the shelling got closer and closer to them, and the urge in every one of them was to run for cover and get out of the structure that was being targeted. The unit's commander, recognizing the situation, calmly joked about the shelling and asked for the unit's barber to use the idle time before any attacks to give him a haircut on the front porch of the house, which he sat through reading a newspaper, which had the calming effect intended and led his men to understand through the simple action that there was no reason to panic.

How many times have you lost your bearing in the face of trying times in your life? The death or sickness of a close friend and/or relative is devastating. The end of a meaningful or serious relationship, loss of a job or business opportunity can be devastating and tear at a leader's ability to maintain bearing. It never meant to me that one had to deny their humanity of genuine expression of emotion. It always meant to express it privately, the same way a parent would in front of a child.   A leader was expected to maintain his or her bearing in front of his or her followers, because it would cause them to panic or create unnecessary anxiety if they saw their leader shaken.

Courage
There are so many authorities on courage that I think the subject is well covered by anyone's review. John F. Kennedy's book Profiles In Courage was but one example of biographical anecdotes of courage and the types of courage great leaders have shown in various circumstances. The military definition of Courage is often cited as the basis of awards, and for great reference material on military courage, I highly recommend that Americans review the citations of the Medal of Honor recipients to understand military courage.

I always understood Courage to mean the courage to speak up and stand up for what you believe in and defend yourself, and the people of who you are leading, and accepting the consequences of your actions and their actions, decisions and beliefs. This concept was stretching the definition the Marines used to define Courage on the battlefield. Whether Courage is standing up in the face withering fire on the battlefield and giving direction to lead infantry men, or it is facing termination of your career or life for sticking to your beliefs, courage is a trait required of a good leader to stand up for what he believes in. It takes courage to face the responsibilities of leadership. Courage means admitting you are human and make mistakes. It also means owning up to your mistakes and facing the consequences of those mistakes and learning from them. Courage also means sticking to your ideals and principles, and not letting fear or someone else's fear or intimidation get into your psyche so that you alter your own personal decisions that lead you off your path defined for yourself. Courage is not equivalent to recklessness or stupidity. It means telling the truth and at times disappointing people when required. Courage is hard to master as a leader because there are so few examples to draw from in many public and private organizations. Courage refers to exercising sound moral and ethical core beliefs taught almost everywhere at an early age and fighting some predisposed natural instincts of some leaders to exploit any and all opportunities from people or from an organization for personal gain.

Decisiveness
This trait may seem pretty self-evident and not require much discussion, but this trait often eludes companies and individual leaders because they require extensive

data inputs before taking action at the cost of others waiting on a decision. On the opposite end of the spectrum, some decision makers jump to conclusions using gut instincts to decide complex issues without weighing all their options, and taking unnecessary risks. This trait requires an individual in charge of others or of multiple resources to carefully consider risks and rewards on all decisions and to do some kind of calculus as to the courses of actions available and their outcomes. This is essential in order to maximize resources and efficiencies for the individual leader and organization. Decisiveness also means sticking to your decisions and defending them to the point that they become indefensible if they are wrong, and you must adjust or make a course correction. Decisiveness does not mean blindly following an incorrect path if there is evidence that supports the decision was wrong and a change must be made. It's hard for many to grapple with making an incorrect decision, but it's a sign of great character to admit you were wrong about a decision, make the necessary correction, and move forward as quickly as possible in a better direction to gain greater success.

In the end all the inputs that were available at the time of a decision should have been weighed, considered and measured, and should have had a deep effect on the decision maker to the point of being able to stick to the decision, but not to the point of obstinacy or stupidity. Many organizations and individuals make decisions without considering the inputs of others, and either thinks they can predict outcomes and see the results of their decisions having adverse effects, yet still pursue their course due to obstinacy or pride rather than admitting their decision was wrong.

Dependability
This trait is also self-evident and doesn't require much discussion. It means to be dependable all the time, and perform your job or role of service to the best of your ability all the time without excuses. Only you know what you are capable of doing in any given task. So many individuals cower behind excuses rather than be dependable to everyone around them, or their organization in which they serve. Dependability also means doing your best, and if your best isn't as good as everyone else around you, then to improve yourself to be as good as or better than all those around you and deliver results. It means showing up prepared, early or on time at the latest, and ready to make a difference and adding your unique value. It is the opposite of doing the least or working at half speed or giving partial effort while working on some personal ambition, goal or agenda that is not core to your specific duty of what you have been committed, hired or commissioned to do. Whether it is to grill hamburgers at a barbecue, keep a bathroom clean, work in or run a multi-billion dollar organization, dependability means doing the best in your role and giving it your all.

Endurance
This trait refers to both the physical and mental endurance required to perform ones job at peak

performance levels. It means making choices to stay healthy, alert and actively engaged both in mind and body. While there is a component of this which is purely physical in concept such as the endurance to march all night and traverse 25 miles in 8 hours of marching with an 80 lb. pack on one's back, or to physically run 3 miles in 18 to 24 minutes, the real trait has to do with the endurance to stay on task until they are logically concluded for the immediate time period. This doesn't mean, work until you drop, it does mean work until you have reached the point that you really can't provide any more practical inputs and let it go until tomorrow to pick it back up. If something can't wait until tomorrow, it means staying up all night and completing whatever it is that needs done, and doing a first rate job at completing it, and having the endurance to stay alert and focused enough to be able to do it. So it means staying away from anything that could cloud your judgment and affect your endurance like alcohol, drugs, or plain lethargy that tends to keep your mind and body out of peak condition to handle the workload at hand. Whether it is changing a tire, running a marathon or restructuring a complex negotiation, you have to have the endurance to see the task through to the end once you start and only stop when it is accomplished before you move on to something else.

Enthusiasm
This trait does not mean that you are expected to be a cheerleader in your organization for everything and everyone. It does mean that you have to effectively and genuinely be enthused about decisions that you have to support even if you don't agree with them personally.

Once you have accepted an assignment as the leader, you must show enthusiasm and communicate with animation to be effective. You can't show that you don't support something more or less by the level of enthusiasm you show, it is in poor taste and a weakness of leadership. If you truly can't back something and can't be enthusiastic about it, or even pretend to be enthusiastic about it, you should consider changing course. If required quit or accept being fired over your lack of agreement. If you're not in a position to quit, then you should be prepared to be fired, and should be focused on finding a new position for yourself as soon as practical. Too many leaders who feign enthusiasm about something they don't support and privately curse the course of action poison themselves as well as the culture or organization they are trying to lead. Doing something you can't support with enthusiasm takes a toll on your individual well-being and is disastrous to the organization. If the organization needs to change their course, and you can't convince them to change, make them fire you over it and replace you with someone who will support that effort, or quit rather than follow along with something someone you can't support or work with enthusiastically. Life is literally too short to do things you fundamentally disagree with.

Initiative
Initiative is not waiting for something or someone to tell you what to do, but to take risks and take action for the benefit of the organization you serve, taking the best course of action you believe is right for the mission. Whether that mission is serving the customer,

the company or the greater cause of helping your community or society, initiative is taking that action which you believe is the correct action. This trait means you don't wait for circumstances to align perfectly up for you to take action, or cover your (or your organization's) mistakes, or prevent mistakes or disasters – that is part of your job in any organization. It means to see ahead and outside of yourself, and take action on whatever needs to be done without consideration for personal gain, and possibly at some risk if it is not your responsibility. Initiative is fixing a problem, or reaching out to prevent a potential problem from occurring, even though no one has specifically designated you in charge of solving the problem or even acknowledged a problem exists. Initiative is not acting for the sake of looking good; it is doing the right thing. If you see something that needs to be done just do it. Leaders demonstrate this trait in most areas of their lives, and you see this everywhere from good Samaritans who stop and help others, or from leaders who step in and solve problems.

Integrity
Integrity is to always be truthful, forthright and straightforward with others. Integrity is easily considered by me the most valuable trait anyone can have, and should be safeguarded and protected. Integrity means to not compromise on the truth for convenience, money, power, fame, or some desire, but to stick to highly moral and ethical values of truthfulness. Integrity means to admit when you make

a mistake and own up to those mistakes and accept consequences for mistakes. Integrity is also the foundation for high moral and ethical values that should not be compromised by anything or anyone. Some great examples of integrity are around us in the children we have raised to tell the truth, and to see them struggle with the consequences of telling the truth, to their own detriment on occasion, but still learn the valuable lessons of how important the truth is to their individual character as leaders.

Knowledge
Knowledge is defined by me as the on-going quest for personal understanding and study of information on subjects not yet mastered and/or understood. It means to educate oneself with both accredited courses of study and practical courses of study. It should be the goal of every leader to not only educate themselves but to encourage others to increase their personal knowledge including technical and non-technical knowledge related to their jobs, their organization, other organizations that compete, their customers, and their customer's customers, as well as the community and society in general where they live. Knowledge in the broad sense of my definition is very similar to seeking to understand, not only people and their perspectives, but also technical aspects of what helps organizations flourish and thrive, and having a genuine interest in increasing ones level of education and understanding.

Loyalty

Loyalty to me is defined as directed in multiple directions, and should be primarily be directed to the overall organization one serves and then in descending order loyalty goes to protecting/helping one's subordinates or direct charges, then to helping peers, and then to helping higher management. Many organizations demand loyalty from their leaders with strict codes of silence and rules within which information cannot be shared for the greater good of the organization; Information is coded or classified as confidential, secret, or top secret, or compartmented as need to know which is reality. Companies have obligations to protect and safeguard their intellectual property, and governments have the obligations to protect and safeguard their secrets and require leaders to operate within the confines of this system, however, loyalty does not mean blindly allowing an organization to violate the values it has defined for itself with interchangeable and interim leaders demanding personal loyalty to them, at the cost of hurting the overall organization, your subordinates or peers. Too many good individuals who basically understand the trait of loyalty to subordinates first have compromised that loyalty to higher management facing the realities of self-preservation. This flaw is a fundamental character weakness in human beings. Politicians demonstrate it in their willingness to stray from their core values of representing their constituents first by allowing special interests to influence their decision making and votes to stay in power. Leaders in companies demonstrate this in pursuit of continued personal enrichment at the cost of their communities and employees' livelihoods. What is worse is that the individuals who truly know better yet compromise their principles and allow organizations to continue pursuits in unfair or unethical competition contribute to the demise of prosperity of everyone.

Tact
Tact is the practice of exercising diplomacy or being nice to people in what you say and how you say it to them. It is the golden rule of treating people like you wish to be treated. I have personally suffered from a lack of exercising a higher amount of tact when voicing my opinions to others and the personal lessons drawn for me is that a little tact can go a long way to accomplish self-promotion goals. However, in the long run, the trait of tact should not compromise your values of integrity, and when you reach the point of no longer being able to voice your dissension with the tact that a situation might require, it is probably better to disengage and re-evaluate where you are working and consider a change. Another way of discussing tact is to consider picking your battles and the ground on which you will fight very carefully if you intend to win. Tact goes a long way in accomplishing a good basis for communication but should never compromise the right thing to say or do.

Unselfishness

Unselfishness is really core to great leadership. Jim Collins in his book Good To Great[1], describes the difference between Level 4 leaders and Level 5 leaders as level 4 leaders take credit for positive results their team delivers, and blame others for negative results; while great leaders or level 5 leaders are the opposite, giving credit to subordinates and others for positive results, while genuinely accepting blame and personal responsibility for negative results of their subordinates. Unselfishness is also the trait that doesn't allow a leader to take advantage of their subordinates for personal gain. Not enough leaders in America today understand the value of this trait, and the law of karma which is the universe's law and is as real as gravity. I can't tell anyone not to be unselfish without first suggesting that they look within themselves for the answers as to whether they want to lead. Leadership comes at great personal sacrifice as history has shown us. Many authors have discussed with profiles and biographies on leaders who sacrificed their personal lives and families for something greater than themselves, serving their people. Gandhi and Jesus are really the two that I consider to be the greatest leaders of all time that exemplified the trait of unselfishness, whether you do or don't believe in God, the examples of these two individual stories are at their core about unselfishness, and if more executives, politicians, union leaders and even criminals understood the value of this leadership trait, I think American companies could

---

[1] Good To Great © 2001 by Jim Collins published by HarperCollins Publishers, Inc., offers excellent reference insight as a former consultant with an insider's look at the characteristics of leaders in companies that made the leap to being great companies.

easily roar back to lead the world into a new era of global collaboration and bring about the end of poverty, crime and war.

[2]Marine Corps' Definitions of the 14 basic traits of leadership from Marine Corps Handbook on Leadership:

Marine Corps Leadership Traits "JJ DID TIE BUCKLE"

The 14 leadership traits are qualities of thought and action which, if demonstrated in daily activities, help Marines earn the respect, confidence, and loyal cooperation of other Marines. It is extremely important that you understand the meaning of each leadership trait and how to develop it, so you know what goals to set as you work to become a good leader and a good follower.

JUSTICE

Definition: Justice is defined as the practice of being fair and consistent. A just person gives consideration to each side of a situation and bases rewards or punishments on merit.

Suggestions for Improvement: Be honest with yourself about why you make a particular decision. Avoid favoritism. Try to be fair at all times and treat all things and people in an equal manner.

JUDGMENT

Definition: Judgment is your ability to think about things clearly, calmly, and in an orderly fashion so that you can make good decisions.

Suggestions for Improvement: You can improve your judgment if you avoid making rash decisions. Approach problems with a common sense attitude.

DEPENDABILITY

Definition: Dependability means that you can be relied upon to perform your duties properly. It means that you can be trusted to complete a job. It is the willing and voluntary support of the policies

---

[2]From
http://www.6mcd.usmc.mil/ftl_site/Handbook/marine_corps_leadership__trait s.htm and http://www.au.af.mil/au/awc/awcgate/awc-read.htm

and orders of the chain of command. Dependability also means consistently putting forth your best effort in an attempt to achieve the highest standards of performance.

Suggestions for Improvement: You can increase your dependability by forming the habit of being where you're supposed to be on time, by not making excuses and by carrying out every task to the best of your ability regardless of whether you like it or agree with it.

INITIATIVE

Definition: Initiative is taking action even though you haven't been given orders. It means meeting new and unexpected situations with prompt action. It includes using resourcefulness to get something done without the normal material or methods being available to you.

Suggestions for Improvement: To improve your initiative, work on staying mentally and physically alert. Be aware of things that need to be done and then to do them without having to be told.

DECISIVENESS

Definition: Decisiveness means that you are able to make good decisions without delay. Get all the facts and weight them against each other. By acting calmly and quickly, you should arrive at a sound decision. You announce your decisions in a clear, firm, professional manner.

Suggestions for Improvement: Practice being positive in your actions instead of acting half-heartedly or changing your mind on an issue.

TACT

Definition: Tact means that you can deal with people in a manner that will maintain good relations and avoid problems. It means that you are polite, calm, and firm.

Suggestions for Improvement: Begin to develop your tact by trying to be courteous and cheerful at all times. Treat others as you would like to be treated.

INTEGRITY

Definition: Integrity means that you are honest and truthful in what you say or do. You put honesty, sense of duty, and sound moral principles above all else.

Suggestions for Improvement: Be absolutely honest and truthful at all times. Stand up for what you believe to be right.

ENTHUSIASM

Definition: Enthusiasm is defined as a sincere interest and exuberance in the performance of your duties. If you are enthusiastic, you are optimistic, cheerful, and willing to accept the challenges.

Suggestions for Improvement: Understanding and belief in your mission will add to your enthusiasm for your job. Try to understand why even uninteresting jobs must be done.

BEARING

Definition: Bearing is the way you conduct and carry yourself. Your manner should reflect alertness, competence, confidence, and control.

Suggestions for Improvement: To develop bearing, you should hold yourself to the highest standards of personal conduct. Never be content with meeting only the minimum requirements.

UNSELFISHNESS

Definition: Unselfishness means that you avoid making yourself comfortable at the expense of others. Be considerate of others. Give credit to those who deserve it.

Suggestions for Improvement: Avoid using your position or rank for personal gain, safety, or pleasure at the expensive of others. Be considerate of others.

COURAGE

Definition: Courage is what allows you to remain calm while recognizing fear. Moral courage means having the inner strength to stand up for what is right and to accept blame when something is your fault. Physical courage means that you can continue to function effectively when there is physical danger present.

Suggestions for Improvement: You can begin to control fear by practicing self-discipline and calmness. If you fear doing certain things required in your daily life, force yourself to do them until you can control your reaction.

KNOWLEDGE

Definition: Knowledge is the understanding of a science or art. Knowledge means that you have acquired information and that you understand people. Your knowledge should be broad, and in addition to knowing your job, you should know your unit's policies and keep up with current events.

Suggestions for Improvement: Suggestions for Improvement: Increase your knowledge by remaining alert. Listen, observe, and find out about things you don't understand. Study field manuals and other military literature.

LOYALTY

Definition: Loyalty means that you are devoted to your country, the Corps, and to your seniors, peers, and subordinates. The motto of our Corps is Semper Fidelis! (Always Faithful). You owe unwavering loyalty up and down the chain of command, to seniors, subordinates, and peers.

Suggestions for Improvement: To improve your loyalty you should show your loyalty by never discussing the problems of the Marine Corps or your unit with outsiders. Never talk about seniors unfavorably in front of your subordinates. Once a decision is made and the order is given to execute it, carry out that order willingly as if it were your own.

ENDURANCE

Definition: Endurance is the mental and physical stamina that is measured by your ability to withstand pain, fatigue, stress, and hardship. For example, enduring pain during a conditioning march in order to improve stamina is crucial in the development of leadership.

Suggestions for Improvement: Develop your endurance by engaging in physical training that will strengthen your body. Finish every task to the best of your ability by forcing yourself to continue when you are physically tired and your mind is sluggish.

Because it is important to always be able to remember the basic leadership traits, the acronym "J.J. DID TIE BUCKLE" is used. Each letter in the acronym corresponds to the first letter of one of the traits. By remembering the acronym, you will be better able to recall the traits.

Back Up Essentials

Your organization has essential elements to it that are the key to its continued existence. If your organization is a bakery, there are kitchen elements like an oven and mixer, bowls, work space and ingredients essential to operating. But even more basic to those essentials, you need customers to buy the baked goods that you produce. If your organization is an office supply business, you need to have on hand inventory that customers need or want, and a way to deliver that inventory, but essential to the business also is customers that need or want those products that you deliver.

I use the analogy of setting up a manual transfer switch to an electrical panel as the key to running any organization, which basically allows any compatible generator to power those essential circuits in a home's electrical system. It is amazing at how simple this concept of backing up essentials actually is to implement, yet people don't see essentials equally. The hardest thing about setting a generator back up system to a house's electrical panel is picking the circuits that you deem essential. Most people go with electrical pumps like well, sump, grinder first, then with refrigerator or other kitchen circuits, then maybe with furnace blower or fan motor system, or other basic essentials, but then when they realize that there is room for much more to be included, they start, to think about lights in different rooms, computers, TVs, DVRs, ceiling fans, etc.,

Which lights are essential in a blackout? Living area lights, basement, garage lights or outdoor deck lights? If you think of your organization in a similar way and start to re-engineer the essentials of what makes your organization run smoothly and look at how you build redundancies as backups to your organization, you find that you must have key elements backed up in the event of a black out, recession or outright depression.

So what's essential to run a business? There are ample business courses to draw from to help anyone start up a specific business and there are very successful franchises that have started and chosen great locations to be successful at whatever business it is they are starting, but to boil it down to the most practical business planning in context to this discussion of what you need and should back up as an essential circuit, like the manual transfer switch in the analogy above, for the purpose of discussion in this book are the following:
Customer strategy, cash-flow strategy, operating capital resource, and infrastructure strategy to attract and retain those customers and the employees necessary to service those customers.

Customer Strategy

What does it take to get and keep customers?

- Sales Generation ability via Internet, Sales Force, Advertising Media Campaigns
- Products/Services segmented by what customers want/need
- Differentiation from others offering similar products/services –price points, bundled services/products
- Programs with repeat business opportunities – keep the customers sticky
- Adding value to customers by providing solutions along with services/products assumed with your organization
- The right people that believe in your organization and its essential abilities to attract and retain customers and can execute on your plans to compete against the larger industry giants

Cash-Flow Strategy

What does it take to generate positive cash-flows?

- Sales Plan that makes sense - is the rate of return acceptable on the cash at risk?
- Pricing Strategy that makes sense - can you really compete and sell a product or service at a comparable price as the larger players and still compete? How do you know?
- Cost containment - can you control costs and be more nimble and flexible than the large industry players?

- Trusted employees who understand your pricing strategy, cost containment and sales plan and can execute on that strategy and execute on your plans.

Capital Resources Strategy
Where are sources of funding for your organization when you need long term capital investments? Take an introspective look at your organization and answer where you will fund the next giant order that comes in.
- Customers progress payments?
- Operating cash flow?
- Investors?
- Bank Loans?
- Owner's Equity?

Infrastructure Strategy
What is your organization's structure or model? How will you provide the key services or products to your customers?
Office space or physical storefront needed?
Virtual Storefront needed with online ecommerce capability in addition to physical space?
Warehouse/manufacturing space needed?
Delivery vehicles needed?
Can you contract manufacturing, warehousing/fulfillment and delivery?
Can you attract and retain employees to work in the environment/infrastructure you've created to support your customers?

Customer Strategy

Sales Generation Ability
Do you already know potential customers who exist that will buy a product or service that you can manufacture or deliver at a better price point than the industry leaders? For example, if you knew that an office supply superstore sells a carton of 5000 sheets of paper for around $40, but buys it for around $32 and will deliver it for free the next business day if someone orders $50 worth of products from an office supply superstore, basically figuring that they can target customers more than likely to buy more than $50 at a time from them and minimize the delivery costs to the same building or location, would you want to compete with them? To compete would mean you'd have to find a supplier of paper who will sell a carton to you for less than $40, and you'd only be able to sell it for around $40, possibly making less on each carton of paper than the industry giant, or you'd have to differentiate your offering in such a manner that people would be willing to pay more than the market $40 to buy that carton of paper from you. It could be that you add value in your delivery service by coming in and picking up old toner cartridges for recycling or offering to shred documents or taking inventory of all their supply cabinets and placing orders for them thus managing their inventory replenishments for them along with the delivery of that carton, or anything that someone else in the industry wasn't willing to do for that price. It would be considered bundling services or

products along with the cost of the paper allowing you to sell it at a higher rate than the market $40.

If you identify a product or service that is needed by a common group of people or organizations, you can segment into pools that can share a common message to all of them about your product or service offering. If you figure out a way to support them on a sustainable basis, then you would have the foundation of a customer base. The idea is to logically think about the needs of particular groups of people or organizations with similar needs that are in the space you wish to compete and go out and talk to them and get the pulse on the level of interest.

Segmenting Customers
One of the best ways known to tackling whether a potential customer population exists is by surveying them. Either schedule interviews with executives of these targeted customers and go to their place of business or talk to them over the phone and just ask them if there is an interest in what you can offer, and if not, why not. The primary function of business development and one of the hardest things to do for most people is get appointments with complete strangers. It is a very important necessity that requires redundant backups if you yourself can't do this. Hire someone who can follow a methodical script or sales process and can provide you with the commitment to follow up with the voluminous tracking details to see who is interested in your particular product or service and why or why not. In the event of the proverbial

blackout, this function must be backed up to continue, or else you will not survive in the long term.

Differentiation

If your customers are potentially everyone on the planet, and you can operate in a virtual environment and actually can get your products or services to every customer on the Internet, then I'm willing to venture that so can just about everyone else in the world offering similar services or products. I'm also willing to guess that the existing industry giants probably have the dominant share of the world's market which is why you should probably work on segmenting a group of customers and sticking to that specific segment of customers. You should be able to achieve the best results by offering something different or specific to that specific segment of customers that you identify as yours. Your differentiation strategy could be as simple as you personally will service all of the customers in a particular zip code or geography that you can locally cover very well and better than the industry giants. This gives you a unique competitive advantage, because even though the other companies may offer that product or service, only your customers will be able to interact with you and derive unique benefit from what you personally or organizationally can offer them in terms of added values.

If your strategy is going to incorporate hiring an outside sales force of either contracted representatives, or employees, just make sure they understand the segmented niche you have identified and they stick

with what works. If you have had success with a
certain customer segment, then grow the opportunities
within that segment to the point of saturation where
you really have maxed out everything you can sell to
that segment before you expand into another
geography or another offering opportunity. Once you
have figured out what works, develop a training
curriculum for ongoing sales representation and
support that maintains the relationships established
with customers and continue to provide value to that
targeted customer base where you have established a
competitive advantage. It further differentiates your
offering and provides insulation from encroaching
competitors who will adjust to compete with your
unique offering.

Repeat Business
Selling Programs that offer repeat business
opportunities to the same customers is one of the best
ways to succeed in a business. Retail grocery stores
have mastered this with reward or bonus cards and
offer an interesting insight for any business to emulate.
One office superstore retailer has taken the concept into
the business to business segment with their Rewards
programs, offering 10% rewards on items purchased at
their copy and print centers. Gross sales margins in
this area have a typical margin of over 75% and are
generally 50% more expensive than businesses going
direct to an industrial or direct commercial supplier
like a printer or promotional products distributor for
that product or service. Commercial printers and
promotional products distributors sell programs where
they offer to pre-print or pre-produce and stock

inventory in warehouses for future fulfillment of custom printed or custom apparel and promotional items like shirts, hats, mugs as well as custom printed envelopes, forms, business cards or marketing materials. This enables them to retain future program sales which contributes to ongoing repeat business, and makes it more difficult for the customer to switch to a lower cost supplier on those items which are already in inventory, because the buyout costs on those items in inventory would be prohibitive. Many commercial manufacturers provide stocking and fulfillment agreements for customers that extend beyond multiple years to secure future returns on initial manufacturing outlay costs. The problem becomes for the customer that if future demand changes for those items, the cost of obsolescence can become very high, and suppliers will consider extending the terms on stocking agreements for new items in exchange for discounted stock buyouts or for complete waiving of stock buyout agreements.

Adding Value
Adding Value to the customer's business is really the key to having a sound customer acquisition and retention strategy. If your offering of products and/or services can add tangible value to your targeted customer, and you can give value either through a bundled offering like adding some service, or through other strategic advantage of geographic location, or greater flexibility than the others in your market space, then you can definitely compete with the industry giants and even beat them at their own game. Large industry giants are very slow to change or even

recognize where a new product or service offering could solidify a necessity for their customer. By thoroughly researching and understanding your customer segment and your customer's customers, you are already one step ahead of the larger organizations who primarily only focus their solutions on specific segments that they have invested to attract and retain, in what is generally a one size fits all approach to doing business with them.

Jeffrey Gitomer is a famous sales trainer and is an authority on sales training, and offers sound advice that is universal in that you should give something of value to get something of value from the universe, he calls it karma.[3] A sound customer strategy includes figuring out what your customers' customers need, and helping your customers deliver solutions more effectively.

Having the Right People
Making decisions on who represents your organization is probably the most important decision a small organization can make, and you should not rush into it without giving considerable thought as to who you put out there as the face of your organization representing your organization to business groups, prospective customers and talking with your existing customers. You must be able to articulate first and foremost what

---

3 The Little Black Book of Connections, ©2006 by Jeffrey Gitomer and published by Bard Press & Little Red Book of Sales Answers © 2005 by Jeffrey Gitomer. Published by Pearson Prentice Hall are two excellent reference training books on the essentials of selling and identifying or prospecting customers.

your vision is for your organization to your segmented customers before you can expect to attract, retain and develop a sales force. If your customer acquisition is as simple as using the Internet, or advertising media to get customers to come to you, then consider that the larger competitors in your market space, probably already have a strategy and budget for this and can duplicate what you are doing. They can't duplicate you and your individual sales pitch to a prospective customer, and/or your trained sales force that believes in your organization.

Backing Up the Essential - Customer Acquisition and Retention Strategy

All of the elements of the customer strategy discussed above should be considered essential to your organization's well-being, and just like you would identify the circuits that you can back up with a manual transfer switch to your electrical panel, only you know what resources you can commit to the effort. Just like transfer switches come in various sizes and configurations, you get what you pay for and invest in. If you only can afford a six circuit transfer switch then you have to really prioritize what's essential to your home electrical panel vs. if you can spend a little more and get a 10 circuit transfer switch which allows you to put four additional circuits into a continuous backup mode if ever needed. Customers are essential to any business, and/or organization, and without them, there is no reason to operate or exist. So this is a key component that needs redundancy in assuring there are customers for your product or service. You can have an acquisition strategy that includes the Internet and a sales force, but you have to have a strategy and a plan that you can execute and backup in case of turnover, or your Internet access crashes. What is your back up plan?

Cash Flow Strategy

Sales Plan

To determine whether your sales plan is sound, ask yourself: Would the money that is going to be put at risk in this venture get better returns sitting in the bank or sitting in a mutual fund, annuity product or buying guaranteed bonds from a bigger more established company with a track record of success? Let's suppose that the guaranteed contract rate of return on the cost of money for your capital investment is 2% to 3% guaranteed for a term of 1 year, will the investment in your planned business venture give you a rate of return equal to or greater than that? Can you prove it with realistic projections of sales, customers that are segmented out for you to sign up? Can you back it up with a solid business plan backed with a coherent sales and marketing strategy that supports your cash flow analysis? Do you understand the cash flow implications of putting this money at risk? Whether it is grandma's money, your retirement fund money or your personal savings, you have to carefully consider how you will fund your venture.

Below is a sample cash flow analysis that shows that the break even occurs at $30,000 in sales, assuming a simple 20% gross margin on sales, and a fixed cost of $6,000 per month, but that if the sales per month don't significantly get above $35,000 per month, then the venture's initial cash investment loses 16% in the first year in the range on an initial cash investment of $25,000. This is just straight math of what flows in and out of the company's cash accounts and doesn't factor anything other than a simple view of cash outlays in the same period that the sales are incurred. Many ventures will confuse the issue further by strategizing to collect payments in advance of incurring costs if possible in a trailing period and hold that cash over in reserves. It is a fact that small businesses must understand that the lifeblood of their survival is positive cash flow, and if your business venture can't generate enough sales to cover the fixed and variable costs associated with supporting the venture, then your money is better left in the bank or under contract for a CD or other guaranteed fund where it is not at risk to lose value.

If you acknowledge that you and your investors are willing to accept the risk of the capital lost in the first couple years to get a new business venture off the ground and into positive cash flow, then you must invest in your customers and sales strategy to generate the sales needed to get the cash flow positive. You can

Projected Cash Flow for Start Up Venture with Initial $25,000 investment						
	Sep	Oct	Nov	Dec	Jan	Feb
BeginningCash on Hand	$ 25,000	$ 19,400	$ 16,400	$ 13,900	$ 13,900	$ 13,899
Sales	$ 2,000	$ 15,000	$ 17,500	$ 30,000	$ 30,000	$ 33,500
COGs Expenses (80%)	$ 1,600	$ 12,000	$ 14,000	$ 24,000	$ 24,000	$ 26,800
Available Cash for ops	$ 25,400	$ 22,400	$ 19,900	$ 19,900	$ 19,900	$ 20,599
Overhead (Fixed)	$ 6,000	$ 6,000	$ 6,000	$ 6,000	$ 6,001	$ 6,002
Ending Cash on Hand	$ 19,400	$ 16,400	$ 13,900	$ 13,900	$ 13,899	$ 14,597
YEAR CONTINUED BELOW:						
Mar	Apr	May	Jun	Jul	Aug	Year Ending
$ 14,597	$ 15,594	$ 17,090	$ 19,085	$ 24,079	$ 24,079	$ 25,071
$ 35,000	$ 37,500	$ 35,000	$ 35,000	$ 35,000	$ 35,000	$ 340,500
$ 28,000	$ 30,000	$ 28,000	$ 28,000	$ 28,000	$ 28,000	$ 272,400
$ 21,597	$ 23,094	$ 24,090	$ 26,085	$ 31,079	$ 31,079	$ 93,171
$ 6,003	$ 6,004	$ 6,005	$ 6,006	$ 6,007	$ 6,008	$ 72,036
$ 15,594	$ 17,090	$ 18,085	$ 20,079	$ 25,072	$ 25,071	$ 21,135

use any number of great applications like Intuit's QuickBooks to help you with the basic accounting functions to manage your business accounting. Beware of unscrupulous accountants who charge for basic services of payroll services and reporting and bundle these into a fee based structure. QuickBooks Professional can do everything anyone needs, and you owe it to yourself and your investors/partners/customers to properly understand the fundamental accounting issues that affect your cash flow and what's at risk if you fail to comply with state and federal reporting requirements essential to any taxpayer. The SBA (Small Business Administration) and IRS provide plenty of free information and a trusted experienced business owner acting as mentor or advisor can provide invaluable assistance to startups. Ask suppliers and prospective customers for professional recommendations regarding certified public accountants, bankers, and attorneys. Treat these professionals well because they can provide invaluable advice and insight to help a startup venture get off the ground. All of your prospective competitors operate on the same generally accepted accounting principles and the giant competitors who are publicly traded report forward looking statements, earnings statements and disclose their balance sheets as public companies accountable to the general public. It would be wise for you to understand how to read and interpret a balance sheet, financial statement of earnings and cash flows and pay particular attention to these financial statements and analysis (that can also be obtained by your investment bankers with opinions on each company) but also pay particular attention to the letters or statements to shareholders of not only your competitor's CEO, but prospective customer's CEO, and prospective supplier's CEO if they are all publicly available.

Pricing Strategy
Can you compete with the industry giants by selling a product or service at a gross profit margin (before expenses like overhead, including commercial space

rent, vehicle or equipment lease costs, fuel, commissions and/or salaries)? That is really the question you have to answer when you look at the industry you are entering. The industry giants all have established operating margins that they expect, and depending on the business make up lower margins with higher volumes of repeated turnover of products in inventory or very high volumes on lower margin products like Wal-Mart. They have mastered bundling low margin items with higher margin items, and have mastered their economy of scale and demanded suppliers bend to their will when it comes to costs and delivery schedules, especially if those items are mission critical for a company like a retail office super store or giant retailer like Wal-Mart. Circuit City Stores, Inc. and other specialty retailers significantly increase their operating margins by selling extended service plans on lower margin technology products. Their associates were trained to bundle higher margin accessories like cables, carry cases, CDRs, DVDs, thumb drives, as well as pushing the extended service plans to customers that walked into the retail stores. Can you compete by offering a specific basket of items that you have made or assembled, that are not carried in Wal-Mart, or another specialty retailer or other industry giants? Sure you can. Direct assembly, manufacturers or wholesale distributors will sell to anyone willing to resell or distribute their products, and you can negotiate with multiple wholesalers to find the perfect niche product bundled with a unique service offering that fits your pricing strategy. A great example is a trade supplier like Grainger which offers accounts to various distributors, plumbers, electricians or to the trade providing a service of putting pumps or electrical supplies into a residential or commercial application. The plumber or electrician will generally add a 20% margin onto the cost supplied by the wholesaler. A commercial printer will also add 20% to the contracted freight or paper costs supplied for the manufacture or printing of a project.

It is for this reason that enterprises like specialty retail office superstores would try to direct as much traffic as possible to their highest margin business which is the copy and print center in their retail stores. The commercial side of one office super store retailer which operates a commercial printing business operates on much smaller gross margins of 14% - 20% for larger customers with manufactured programs of stocked printed forms and labels, and a higher 22% - 30% in middle-market of customers for corporate identity products of business cards, letterheads and envelopes that are customary for every business which is still far better than the -1% of gross margin on computers and laptops offered at their retail stores. Technology is used as a tease to get customers in the door at one office super store retailer where the sales staff focuses on creating an inspired buying environment where customers will feel good about buying higher margin items while in the store to purchase the bargain computer on sale.

Understanding the pricing strategy of your competitors is imperative to understanding whether you can compete in the market space with those industry giants. Go back to the example used earlier of a carton of 5000 sheets of paper selling for around $40 and costing everyone around $32. Can you compete by selling the carton of paper at $38 or $39? Why not, if you're also able to bundle higher margin items along with it, or consider charging $41 or $42 for a carton of paper by bundling a better service offering of allowing customers to receive same day orders if ordered before noon, or some similar competitive offering the industry giants just wouldn't offer.

You can check the soundness of your pricing strategy by surveying your competition, run targeted marketing campaigns to specific customer segments offering sale prices to see what price point works, and more importantly what price point doesn't work. Understanding and developing an effective pricing strategy is a key element like cash flow that is essential to whatever product or service you wish to offer to compete with the industry giants. Pricing strategies have to make sense over time. Companies that put forth a strategy of selling a product or service below their actual costs to make or buy and deliver the items lose money over time and either go out of business because of inability to continue funding the loss or they successfully gain the market share they intend to gain but then are forced to raise prices to stay in business. Any business can amortize the cost of products or services sold in terms of selling that product or service on a longer term contract. For example, to purchase a smart phone independent of a call and data plan could cost $250 but when activated with a two year contract with a carrier at an average of $50/month that $250 smart phone now has ended up costing $1200. Large companies and especially industry giants who try to create monopolistic empires count on their customers not to "cherry pick" or purchase items in un-bundled increments or shop too carefully and take the path of convenience. If you need groceries, and you see that shampoo is available or motor oil in the case of the mega retailers selling it all in one location, they count on consumers to pick up multiple items while shopping for grocery items. There is no reason you can't offer a similar price strategy for products and services over a multi-year arrangement as well, bundling convenient or like services together, but the difference is you can deliver the products or services to your customers in a basket with a bow and charge a premium price for the service.

The way to beat the industry giants is to offer additional values that the large giants just aren't willing to offer and to set a price accordingly that yields enough net operating margin to operate in the positive cash flow range that will position long term success. A price strategy is as essential as cash flow and everyone in your organization must understand it, promote it, and live the service or product offering.

Cost Containment Strategy
If you are defining what essentials your organization needs to "back up" like a circuit on an electrical panel then establishing a culture of containing costs to the bare minimum is necessary to compete with the large competitors in your industry. The large companies have figured out since the crash of their stock prices along with the majority of stocks in the US in 2009, that

cash and capital is not unlimited and costs require vigilant management. These giants are smart enough to demand more from employees and net returns on assets purchased in faster return cycle than ever before. Industry giants with cost controls in place will not expend a dime without a formula that provides positive returns through various models that prove the investment is worthwhile. The industry giants can afford to pay ivy league educated managers and professional consultants from top tier accounting and consulting firms to develop analysis models for them as part of their process of due diligence on the launch of a new product, service offering, or direction to include acquisition or merger, and they won't pursue that course of action unless there is a positive return on that investment. What they lack in executing on these great plans is people like you. They are not able to attract and retain entrepreneurial minded employees who view costs and productivity as essential elements of long term survival and the ability to thrive. Small family owned business enterprises with personal fortunes at risk understand costs better than anyone and unless their cash and income is unlimited (which in some families it could be), most small businesses expect a return on the investments made in operating a business. This return can only come from developing a culture of keeping all costs to a minimum.

This culture comes from the top down. If the owners inadvertently create an environment of the "haves" and "have-nots" in their organization, without offering equity sharing to employees at all levels of the organization, it is a missed opportunity to create a great organization. The large industry giants have figured this out and attempt to establish a culture of ownership by providing stock equity grants to management. It is a good idea to emulate this approach unless you can convince friends and family to volunteer their services and still remain loyal to your organization and help you create the culture that keeps costs at the bare minimum. Employees that are invested in the organization's future tend to understand cost containment strategy and will support owners and manager's decisions and will contribute far greater contributions than employees who are paid a simple wage or salary for providing a service. Without a sense of future ownership or stake in the company or organization, why would they feel like it is their business as well at stake competing with the industry giants?

As part of your cost containment strategy it would behoove you to implement a logical and ethical procurement process for everything your organization requires. Either manually build your own model or acquire one off the shelf from any number of sources that provide software as a service "SaaS" solution that can build a simple purchasing model for those items that are mission critical for you to operate. Building your own model is very time consuming to get multiple bids on every purchase from paper clips, ink and paper to vehicles, electricity, coffee, fuel, temporary labor or leased equipment. It is not only necessary but vital that you stick to a rigorous procurement process and make informed decisions about spending any cash which is

really the lifeblood that is necessary to continue
operating in the long term.

Obtaining the Right Employees
So, if it is essential to actively have a strategy for cash
flow, pricing and cost containment, then the last but
certainly not the least essential element that you must
back up is a source for the best possible people to work
in your organization. Where do you obtain the best
people to help you execute on your organization's
vision? Look around. Always be recruiting. I'm not
suggesting you poach your customer's best people (at
least not without their acknowledgement and blessing),
or that you go out and poach your competitor's best
people, because that will only start a war with your
competitors. I am suggesting that you always remain
open to recognize talent and find a way to make an
opportunity attractive enough for them to want to join
your organization. Whatever the essence of your belief
and value system, it should be core to your
organization's mission and values. It could be that you
aim to be recognized as a socially responsible partner in
your community, specific charity or cause that you
support, or it could be that you believe in something
that others also believe in, whatever it is; attracting like-
minded people is a starting point for recruiting into
your organization.

Recruiting or retaining great employees is as essential
to your organization as cash flow. When it comes right
down to apples to apples comparisons with the giant
industry competitors that you are going head to head

against, the real differentiator is the people your customers interact with, see and touch on a daily basis. Employees of larger competitors can receive cash and stock incentives that the industry offers. However without a core belief that the larger organization is the employee's long term future with perfect alignment to the employee's personal values and belief systems, it is unlikely the larger company's employees will be able to compete with your employees. The genuine sincerity and harmony that your customers will not only see, hear and feel, but will recognize from your employees will differentiate your team from those larger company's employees offering incentives for customers to switch. Your employees are as much the lifeblood of your organization as your cash flow. Treat them fairly, treasure their contributions, thank them regularly, reward them with the most that you can and honor your values which hopefully are aligned with their values.

The key is don't settle for employees who don't share your vision, passion and aspirations. You will not be able to execute on any of those things without employees willing and able to execute on them. With that said, have an active and ongoing reading and continuous education strategy for your employees. All employees from the operations employees in customer service, shipping and receiving, to the sales and marketing representatives have to be willing and able to learn and improve themselves in order to help you execute on your plan to compete against the industry giants. Those organizations have invested in training their people and make investments in ongoing continuous training. You also have to understand that the best possible team supporting your customers must continuously improve and add value for your customers. If you can afford tuition reimbursement as a benefit, make it a priority, and recruit from the business schools around you. If you can attract top tier schools talent that share the same beliefs and values as your own, to join your organization by offering internships or future equity based on growth (to save on costs), you may just find the hidden talent that will help your organization reach heights well beyond your expectations and possibly innovate something well beyond what the larger industry competitors can offer. More than likely, however, the top tier schools have large companies offering much greater incentives than you can afford to attract and retain the graduating students of their business school programs. In order to find potentially great talent you should seriously consider looking at the vocational schools and adult education schools for top talent. There are so many great accredited online educational programs readily available now for working adults that the opportunities to find experienced, highly educated and talented employees is right there within the job boards of these schools, such as American InterContinental University, Strayer University, University of Phoenix and Kaplan University as well as the community colleges and state universities offering certificates and accredited degrees.

Schools are an excellent resource pool to find and attract the talent needed for specific customer research projects, as well as innovating new ideas that you can put to use at a fraction of the cost of what the larger competitors in your industry would even consider trying. Larger companies tend to ignore these great resource pools of working adults in school because they don't need to look beyond their existing applicant pool. Large companies receive so many applicants willing to work for these larger well-known brands that they can be very selective. Large companies narrowly focus on the individual candidate's skills or experience aligned to the specific job requirements sought for a specific position. There is hardly concern placed on the individual values and traits that might fit the overall organization. Larger companies myopically overlook good people who are making investments in themselves to improve their skills and very likely have transferable skills that can be taught by you and your organization because they don't have to invest as much in training someone and can get a faster return on the investment of the new hire, and by and large larger companies regard human resources generally as a commodity that are interchangeable like equipment and need to be managed with generalists or specialists. This dehumanizing relationship between large organizations with the owners and senior executive leaders far removed from the people who do the work every day and have the closest interaction with the customer every day is really a competitive advantage that smaller companies have over their larger competitors.

In his 2001 book Good To Great[4] Jim Collins cited the example of great companies understanding that it is not

---

[4] Good To Great, © 2001, Jim Collins Chapter 3 "First Who Then What"

enough to "have the right people on the bus", but really need to "have the right people in the right seat on the bus." The assumption is that having the right people hired to fit the company will make the company great because no matter what direction the company's ownership decides to go, these great people will make the outcome successful. Having them all in the right positions to impact the company makes the company great. Collins profiled as an example, Circuit City Stores, Inc., as one of the great companies that outperformed the S&P 500 which was his benchmark of a great company. Circuit City Stores, Inc. (CC) was delisted from NYSE in November 2009 and liquidated assets after it failed to find a buyer, and in hindsight Collins was right about the people in a company, but he did not qualify his assertion to include that having the right people in the right seats meant they had to have the ability to stop the bus from driving off of a cliff which is what happened when Circuit City's managers allowed the senior leaders to take the company in the wrong direction and fire their commissioned sales force which was their main differentiator to rival Best Buy. Those leaders were from the top tier business schools in America, and were not exactly the "roll up their sleeves" and dig right into understanding and solving the problems and concerns of their employees. The working adults going to school at night supporting a family and considering career changes or improvement of their life's work and situation are exactly the type of people you want to put in your organization. Especially if they believe in your organization and you believe in them, and are willing to help them reach their goals. The law of karma applies. Give them value and equity in your company's future, and they can help you achieve the goals you need to compete with the larger industry competitors.

Obtaining the right people for your organization is essential to your existence and ability to compete with the large competitors. If you can't compete in direct pay, offer up future equity stakes as indirect pay or variable merit based pay incentives that are congruent with your beliefs, vision and organization's goals. If you don't believe in sharing the wealth of your future success with your employees as stakeholders and only view them as an interchangeable commodity of human resources, reconsider your position, because your customers are loyal to those employees and prefer doing business with them and don't like turnover.

Have a performance management system that does not dehumanize your employees with a meaningless numerical ranking that says doing a great job is expected of everyone. Be consistent in recognizing your employees for the work they do but don't have to do as well as they do. Reward performance and talent with the best compensation or equity that you can offer. Don't allow this to become an expectation or entitlement for everyone. Equity incentive and merit pay should be earned, not given out for time in service. Be sure to make it possible and achievable to earn it, and make it of real tangible value to compete with the larger industry competitors for top talent.

Performance management also means that if employees are not performing well enough to your standards make it possible and clear to them how to improve, and act decisively if there is not a fit with the employee. Make sure to make other employees and customers aware of the decision being made and why, and always be justified and on the right moral and ethical side of any terminations of employees. In the case when an employee departs for other opportunities, or you have to dismiss them, treat it like a treasured member of your family departing for better opportunities, because that's what it should be to your organization. Have a bench of applicants or other employees ready to cover for that individual just as you would if individuals went on vacation. Performance management and recruiting strategy of people is essential.

Having a pool of candidates that you would consider hiring is as important to your organization as cash flow, pricing and cost containment strategies. These elemental essentials are the lifeblood and are like the essential circuits that you have to pick and should be prepared to back up for your organization and be able to manually switch to a backup generator if the main power goes out and you are looking to continue your business operations. If you think you have an adequate strategy for each of these essentials and can back them up with some redundancy in case your primary sources fail, then you should be well prepared to compete with the larger competitors in whatever industry you enter.

Operating Capital Resources Strategy

While customers progress payment and cash flow is the ideal source for on-going operational capital resources, it is not very realistic to think that any new or existing business in this environment at the time of this writing can actually sustain themselves for the long term without a sound source for operating capital. Even a small business is going to need significant capital resources or access to capital to compete with the industry giants. The Small Business Administration has a wealth of great and free information available regarding funding sources from government grants and private lenders who work with government backed guarantees. If not sure where to look, just do a Google search for "microloans" and you will see multiple sources for capital. Many states, county or municipalities in the US have even gone so far as to establish economic development councils made up of established business leaders including commercial banks providing access to capital resources. Using government funded incubators with access to research university resources, in turn have access to capital for businesses that fit their investment strategies. Whether it is attracting manufacturing or technology sector jobs, grant providing bodies can provide excellent capital investment suggestions and resources for businesses with big ideas that are congruent with their particular investment strategy with public-private sources of money.

So what if your business isn't eligible for grants, incubators or investment strategies of banks for the capital you need? You have to ask yourself whether your business model is serving a need or providing a product that is essential to businesses or consumers. If it is not, but there are existing players that are well established and making a proverbial killing, and you want to compete with them, there is a way to compete, but you have to have access to funds to get your business over the entrance barriers and clear an ongoing hurdle rate of the cost of money. That money for most businesses comes from the owner's pockets. Funds come from either pooling funds from family, friends, or private wealthy individuals willing to invest in the owner, or investors who like the idea of the entity trying to compete and may be willing to help. People don't hand money out to anyone without expecting a return on the investment, and good people with even the best ideas won't accept putting someone else's money at risk because if their ideas fail to materialize results, it is not easy to face family, friends, or those wealthy individuals and apologize for the failures. So if you are going to ask mom and dad, or grandma or the wealthy uncle to back your great idea, you better understand the returns that you can deliver to them and make it more attractive than just keeping their money in the bank at minimal or no risk. If you cannot in good conscience ask your friends and family to invest their money or sweat equity volunteering to help your business get off the ground, then you should really think twice about your business venture and idea.

If you decide to back your business with your personal assets which are required by most banks or suppliers extending capital or credit, then fully understand what you are putting up at risk. Don't go into any venture without completing the basic calculus of what your personal rate of return on your investment is going to be based on sound logical critical thinking. If you are so committed to a venture and it is truly your passion, or core belief that you cannot or will not be happy and fulfilled in life unless you put your personal assets, time and energy at risk of losing it all, in the pursuit of this venture, then by all means jump in with both feet. Just have enough capital available to clear the initial hurdle rates of entry into the industry you are going into. Treat cash like it was as precious as the greatest thing in the world you treasure, because you must find ways to protect and safeguard spending it, and finding other sources to fund your venture. You can issue promissory notes for cash to strangers to invest and guarantee them a particular rate of return on their investment. Investment banks can assist if the opportunity and rate or returns are large enough. Your business will have to be large enough or uniquely different to stand out from the others in your field or industry to attract any established venture capital resources, other than your personal network. Whatever sources of capital you find make sure that you understand the value of cash and capital at the net present value. You must understand that the value of $1 today is different than the future value of that dollar due to natural inflation where that dollar buys less. Ask for qualified help to get your venture off the ground and continuously improve on your wealth positioning and management. Someone with an education or experience owning and operating a business can be a treasured wealth of knowledge about sources of capital. Look for good advice and educate yourself on money if you are not an expert already on how to raise cash or have you don't have ample resources of cash to fund your venture's ongoing operations for 6 months to one full year. Just like having a six month personal rainy day fund that you can access if you lose a job or have a major emergency expenditure, your business venture needs to have the same plan for capital backed up on the proverbial circuit to the manual transfer switch like the rest of your essentials of loyal customers and employees, cash flow strategy and infrastructure strategy.

Infrastructure Strategy

The final element for discussion that any business needs backed up as an essential element to compete with the industry giants is a sound infrastructure strategy. Infrastructure refers to the physical and virtual facilities required to operate your business or organizational venture. Can you operate it out of your basement, garage or kitchen? Is zoning permitted in your residence to operate a business or other non-residential operation out of your residence? Do you need vehicles, warehousing, and/or manufacturing and office space? How much of an infrastructure investment is really needed to compete? And what is the minimum fixed cost you can manage? If you're going to put up a retail operation, is the location logical and conducive to giving you a competitive advantage? If your strategy is to compete with larger industry giants do you have to pay more for premium space locations over the competition that may not have to or be willing to? If you can operate virtually can you develop virtual solutions that are more competitive in offering than others in your industry or field?

If it is a crowded and fragmented field in which you compete, is there confusion about who leads because of vast fragmented numbers and wide ranging participants all over the world? What infrastructure strategy helps you to compete? Geographically putting up your operation in a particular region could be a competitive advantage to corner a local or regional market. Do you have unique patents or intellectual property that gives you competitive advantage? If not, can you research and develop them and build infrastructure around them to help you compete?

If geographical or locational advantage is not part of your infrastructure strategy because you can compete in a virtual environment, your infrastructure strategy must include all the software, hardware and employees needed to compete with the industry giants and be backed up with redundancies in case people call out sick, servers crash or software doesn't deliver on the expectations. What can you do to protect your enterprise infrastructure?

Do you understand the threats to the industry that you are entering or competing in from existing competitive rivalry, threats of new entrants, substitution, the bargaining power of buyers and/or suppliers? These five forces identified by Harvard Business School's Michael Porter (also known as the 5 force analysis)[5] is the fundamental view that is essential to any owner going into a new venture. You must fully understand an industry's participants and the infrastructure needed in any size enterprise trying to compete against the industry leaders or stand out and differentiate with competitive advantage. Advantage comes from having better trained and more loyal employees, innovation, new technologies that can substitute what existing competitors currently possess or can easily get without significant development or licensing costs to compete. Larger industry giants usually would have huge economies of scale and access to capital resources, which is their competitive advantage, but anyone can compete within an industry if they set up the right mix of offering that helps to minimize the competition's advantage.

Again, this goes back to having a sound strategy in identifying, attracting and retaining the customers that will want you to work with them over the competition while maintaining a sound cash flow strategy, capital resources, and infrastructure. These are essentials to creating an enterprise that is going to compete with the industry leaders. Whether your venture is providing a service or manufacturing products, they all tie together as the foundation to an organization. They must be backed up with redundancy like the analogy of

---

[5] Competitive Strategy: Techniques for Analyzing Industries and Competitors © 1980 by Michael Porter published by First Free Press and considered the definitive work on business strategy in the world's business schools.

selecting which circuits to put on a manual transfer switch in your home to back up those circuits in the event of a power outage, so you can continue to function smoothly until your normal power source is restored.

The understanding required to compete with the industry leaders with your particular competitive advantage is that before you get too far down the road with any venture, be sure to back up the essentials of a sound customer strategy, cash flow strategy, operating capital resources, and infrastructure strategy that will give you the ability to sustain yourself, and weather any economy and build an enterprise that will last.

Selling

There are many great resources available to the modern enterprise of any size for great advice on sales training to hone an organization's sales skills. Among the best for any solutions based entrepreneur is the work <u>Selling to the C-Suite</u>[6], as well as Jeffrey Gitomer's sales training reference books and materials available everywhere[7]. If you aren't familiar with either, I recommend to any owner or sales manager that you invest in that material for your sales force. Even if your plan is to contract a sales force or directly hire a sales force, the key concepts of understanding solutions based selling and sales are essential to getting the right salespeople into your organization to represent your products or services. Solution based selling is the latest trend in management which most large enterprises across industries have adopted and teach at various levels or degree. There is no magic solution that generates sales other than the right people delivering the right message at the right time to the right

---

[6] <u>Selling To The C-Suite What Every Executive Wants You To Know About Successfully Selling To The Top</u> © 2009 by Nicholas A.C. Read and Stephen J. Bistritz, published by McGraw Hill. This book provides excellent research background, tools and models for solution based selling that every entrepreneur involved in selling needs to know.

[7]<u>The Little Black Book of Connections</u>, ©2006 by Jeffrey Gitomer and published by Bard Press & <u>Little Red Book of Sales Answers</u> © 2005 by Jeffrey Gitomer. Published by Pearson Prentice Hall are two of the best-selling sales books packed with tips on selling, and prospecting for new customers

audience. It is up to the sales professionals to understand this and the basic fundamentals of selling and sales cycles of the products and/or services being sold to deliver results.

The only numbers that really matter in the end is the sales generated in a given period and that is based on the size of the pipeline that can be converted to sales and the activity levels that the sales force is generating to derive the results. It is different for every organization product and/or service offered and the particular sales cycle as to how quickly the results come in, but invariably the results are all based on this simple truth of what is the sales triangle which must be measured for optimum results:

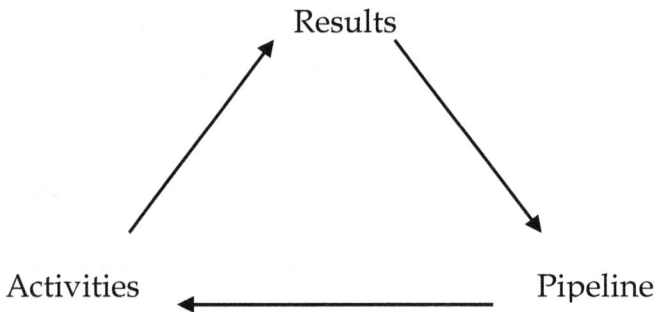

Results

Activities

Pipeline

The basic rule of professional selling is to look at the sales triangle or the three legged stool that must be in harmony to remain in balance. Measuring sales results without looking at the relational aspect of the other two corners of the triangle necessary to drive sales results is a huge misstep. Results are usually dependent on the other two. If you want better results, first look at the pipeline, if it isn't large enough to sustain the results desired look at the activities and see if they are the right volume, focus and type of activities that will drive the results desired.

If one of the legs of a three legged stool is short or unstable then usually the stool is not stable either, and so it is with any organization dependent on sales results to sustain ongoing operations.

Before you can get results of sales, you have to make appointments, present quotes and deliver a promise or a product that the customer accepts which creates a sale. A pipeline is all the open opportunities that you have identified as potential sales and categorized into appropriate buckets or stages ranging from: Gathering info on a prospective customer you just heard about or met to being in the process of quoting some deliverables, to having closed and won the sale and you are awaiting payment or closed and lost the sale. You have to measure your progress. There are ample database applications readily available with MS Excel or Access to cloud software like Salesforce.com that makes it very easy for an organization to keep track of their sales in relation to activities, pipeline and results.

Salesforce.com is one of the premier cloud based applications that works well at tracking every level of the sales triangle, and is easy enough to customize to just about any organization, and is used by most of the large enterprises if they don't have their own in house tools already developed. Whatever system you develop or deploy, just make sure you understand it and that your sales force lives by it.

A good sales representative usually demonstrates the traits consistent with a positive attitude, understanding the value of maintaining positive relationships and personal connections. They usually also follow a structure whether it is derived by your organization's formula or their own formula for success. They remain highly organized and methodical in their approach to solving a problem, remain open to ideas on how to improve their sales performance, and remain competitive if not with other sales people than with themselves to improve their earnings.

There are solutions based selling fundamentals that are well established and taught by many organizations. I have adopted a solutions based formula that is transferrable and easily modified for any organization and industry outlined here:

Selling Fundamentals for all Sales Representatives:

1. Know The Product or Service Being Sold
2. Know the Required Mechanics of Necessary Sales Activities
3. Measure Open Pipeline Results Frequently
4. Compare Sales Results Against Benchmarks
5. Tweak Sales Activities to Effect Pipeline Management to Drive Desired Results

Know the Product or Service Being Sold
Once you have the right individuals selected to represent your organization, your first step is to educate those representatives about the uniqueness of

your organization, products and services, value proposition, competitive landscape and basic SWOT analysis (teach reps to leverage competitive strengths, minimize weaknesses, improve on existing competitive opportunities, mitigate any threats) skills related to your products and/or services.

These fundamentals are what experienced professional sales people will look for from your organization to guide them along with marketing materials that are developed or will need to be developed to support their sales efforts. It is not enough to simply provide material to sales people. It is imperative you practice their delivery of this material with you or other staff in your organization. Introduce them to friendly or established and well known loyal customers or other partners that can provide you honest feedback about a particular representative's strengths and weaknesses in a real selling situation and environment. This provides a foundation from which to develop individuals to improve on their current skill sets, and also provides you the opportunity to build a high performing sales organization.

Know the Mechanics of Necessary Sales Activities

Experienced sales professionals will be organized and understand the value that time wasted is the equivalent to money wasted. Effective salespeople know good time management skills come with the job. The research done by Stephen J. Bistritz and Nicholas A.C.

Read in their book <u>Selling to the C-Suite</u>[8] proved what most sales professionals who reach the ranks of being trusted advisors already know, which is the fact that doing adequate research on prospects is the price of admission to get appointments with prospects. If your sales representatives are new to the role of professional sales, you have to educate them on this fundamental truth that their time is worth tangible money and information is king.

It is not enough to show up for a first appointment and ask "What do you do here? So I can help design a customized solution or program for you". Sales professionals have to differentiate themselves by showing up on their first engagement either over the phone or at the actual first appointment armed with more information and frame the questions by asking the questions this way, "I see that your company sells X products or Y services to customers A, B & C, and that you were awarded best place to work in ABC county, what makes this such a great place to work and how does your company do it? Or why are these priorities that your CEO spoke about last month so important to your organization right now?" A discussion and a dialogue in that first appointment has to take place

---

[8] Selling to the C-Suite: <u>What Every Executive Wants You to Know About Successfully Selling to the Top</u> ©2010 by Stephen J. Bistritz and Nicholas A.C. Read conducted original research specific to what made salespeople effective. Their research definitely illustrated that effective sales people were the ones who researched their prospective customers prior to showing up or engaging the prospective customer, making it clear beyond anecdotal evidence that salespeople were better received by prospective customers if they knew about their prospective customer's business issues and concerns prior to engaging the prospective customer.

setting the tone that not only are your salespeople somewhat familiar with your customer's business, but they are genuinely interested in it, and would sincerely like to help in whatever way possible. The differentiator of values is what will set your sales organization apart from the competition. If your sales professionals only care about making a sale, then it will show in results that look like roller coaster numbers month after month vs. steady progressive growth.

Whatever metrics that are required to achieve the sales results your organization needs, set up a measurable action plan to drive results tied to the right activities. In other words in a simple transactional sales environment, the law of probabilities and statistics applies to the point that mathematically you can prove within some varying degree of accuracy that 'x' number of calls in a week will generate 'y' number of appointments, that will yield to 'z' number of quotes generated, which in turn will lead to 'z/2' or 'z/3' orders depending on price and varying factors of how the quote was derived and presented which will lead to tangible sales results in dollars gained.

In order to vary the results, you would alter varying factors to your equation such as the gross margin percent of a quoted price, or you would need to increase the frequency or number of appointments in a given time period to affect the results. Selling is not for everyone, but everyone can sell and has the ability to learn how to sell if they understand the fundamental of selling which at its core is solving a problem for a customer.

In the cases where the customer doesn't even know they have a problem or may not have a current problem in sight, a good sales professional will help a prospective customer see beyond their current situation and imagine a future outcome with their solution improving their overall situation. A good sales professional helps the customer visualize what an alternative outcome could look like that would take the prospective customer to an even better state. Good sales people genuinely strive to improve things within the customer's organization, and not just sell whatever solution they happen to offer through your organization which makes the best salespeople very valuable to customers and you.

Fundamental mechanics of selling activities include qualifying which prospective customers will fit your optimal solution and would already be part of your organizational mission, vision and infrastructure. The next step would be setting the appointments with prospects followed by the steps necessary to prepare for the first appointment, second or follow up appointments and presenting a quote or solution. This is then followed by the last step which is as important as the other steps which is *following up* on a continuous basis to keep competitors from getting in between your organization and your customer and establishing new relationships.

Qualifying Prospects in the Solutions Business

Know your geography and know where the prospective customers are located. Pay attention to building directories with new tenants moving in and out and seek active referrals from customers or networking associations. Know what your prospects do and who their customers are as well. Know which organizations your prospects belong to or network in and join those associations to try to make a connection or get a referral to a prospective customer.

Understand industries that have common needs or threads that you can tie together to your organization's solutions. For example, healthcare is a broad group of prospective customers that include large group managed, or independent regional hospitals, private practitioners, and pharmacies. They all have employees, vendors, partners, customers and suppliers that have needs from integration of information systems or modernization of processes or equipment to better conditions to improve their overall offering. The point is there are common needs to this industry group that could be related to information privacy or other regulatory compliance, risk management, communication management or other commonalities that can be offered by your organization's solutions based service or product to other customers who may share the need for similar solutions.

Similarly customers can be segmented by industry types to better understand where to fit in a common solution that you may be offer including: non-profits, architectural and engineering, construction, technology, retail, legal, hospitality, associations, faith-based churches and schools, public and private education, manufacturing and distribution to name just a few industries that can be segmented and qualified for your solution.

At a minimum to qualify a prospect you need to make a presentation before you can get a sale. You must know that you have identified the correct company, decision maker, and that they have the authority to say yes to meet the spend requirement you are proposing.

Qualifying prospective customers can take place on the phone or through the Internet or in person canvassing by just doing research and asking questions. Conversations on the phone or in person are more productive basing 80% of a successful outcome on how the sales representative asks something and 20% based on the actual words used to qualify the prospect to set up a future appointment. I will also mention that sales can also be generated through clever automated marketing and brand advertising tools like multiple media outlets, or specifically written email auto-responders, email marketing and general Internet marketing which is effective to a targeted audience.

Generally if you are competing against an industry giant, you're going to best differentiate with yourself being the difference, and doing everything possible to get in front of prospective customers and get your message in front of them. The larger companies have better multi-media advertising and Internet marketing capabilities and they have the advantage of an established well-known brand. So you will need to do more to overcome the larger giants competing for the same prospective customer while you are building your own brand. Relying solely on one medium for advertising or automated and clever marketing gimmicks is not enough.

Jeffrey Gitomer recommends giving something of value to a prospective customer before asking anything of that prospective customer. Giving value could be providing the prospective customer's CEO a sales lead as an example. Gitomer goes so far as to suggest giving out two sales leads before asking for an appointment or meeting. It is great advice and definitely works.

Appointment Setting
Every sales professional knows what their organization's value proposition is, and if you have trained them well they can practice delivering that value proposition in a simple 30 second presentable speech, as if the sales rep just bumped into their decision maker in the elevator, or at the counter at the café in a chance encounter. Setting the appointment for sales professionals comes down to quickly getting to the point about why the prospect needs to meet with the sales professional. The value proposition is the primary basis to get that first appointment. Great sales professionals will not take no for an answer over the phone when it comes to getting an appointment with a decision maker they want to meet with. It can take considerable effort just to get to the qualified decision maker on the phone or in person, including preliminary steps like sending a few letters and emails

indicating that you wish to speak with them in the future so your name is recognizable when you actually call that decision maker for an appointment.

The difference between a good sales professional and a great sales professional is the ability to overcome objections smoothly and effectively to get the desired results of a meeting.

There are basically only a few standard objections common throughout almost all industries including the following:

- Send information in the mail or email
- I'm too busy
- You're too expensive
- I don't have anything to talk to you about right now
- I'm happy with my current providers
- I'm not interested in talking to you
- My vendors match prices from competitors like you
- I have a long relationship with my current providers
- I've never heard of you
- You can't meet my needs
- I am under contract with someone else

Almost all objections encountered by sales professionals on the phone like the ones listed above can be overcome with standard conditioned responses from trained sales professionals including responses like:

1. Clarifying Response – Give their objection right back to the prospect on the phone and ask them to clarify what they mean

and rebound the objection back to the prospect for a more detailed response.

2. Case Study Response – Respond to their objection by citing another customer or situation with the same objection and offer testimonial, anecdotal or case study evidence that supports your pitch and the reason for the meeting. Offer to bring this written material or send it in advance of meeting to confirm the appointment. Cite how other customers felt the same way about not wanting to meet, but were glad they met with you afterward.

3. Affirming Response – Respond with a positive affirmative statement indicating "Without understanding what I can do for your co., it's exactly why we need to meet."

In a one day training workshop, sales professionals can master these techniques with personal creative and humorous responses that build instant rapport, generate conversations, get appointments and drive sales results.

Appointments

First Appointments have different objectives than second or third appointments where the sales professional is going back to present a quote and solution, or follow up on the first appointment.

First Appointment objective

The objective of the first appointment in a solution selling environment is to figure out what the customer does, how they order whatever product or service your organization provides and really see if there is a fit between the two organizations. Near 90% of the first appointment should be the customer doing the talking, and your sales professional basically interviewing the customer with questions digging for answers that can lead to understanding the prospective customer's potential to work together. The price for admission into this first meeting is the sales professional having already done the homework on the prospective customer, the individual who they are meeting with and knowing key things about the company and industry including the competitors and forces at work in that customer's industry. At the very least, you should know that customer's industry, competitors, customers served, mission, vision or purpose for being, and individual's title and role in the organization, even if you do a Google search in the parking lot 15 minutes before your appointment, so you or your sales professional differentiate from the countless other sales professionals calling on the prospective customer.

There are solid techniques that are established and used by the best sales organizations consistently to derive solutions. In Selling To The C-Suite, Bistritz and Read, point out the chemical definition of the word "solution" defined as the solute or substance that is dissolved in a solvent to form a solution. It is appropriate for sales professionals in the solution selling environment to fully understand that concept early in the first appointment or meeting with a prospective customer. In making lemonade as cited in Bistritz and Read's book, they liken the crystal powder packs of lemonade as the solute, and water as the solvent, when combined produce the solution lemonade. By the same definition of solution, individuals could create a toxic solution by combining two incompatible components of a solvent and solute. If you are not a good fit for the needs of the prospective customer, or vice versa, then it is best to move on up front and understand that it's just not a good fit, and your solution while might be as effective as whatever solution the customer has, is just not a fit for you or the prospective customer. Your sales representatives must fully understand that even though everyone's capabilities or solvent may be compatible with the customer's needs or solute, your sales professionals have to present the offering in such a way as to convince the prospective customer that the combined solution of your organization will be better overall.

Hold specific workshops that build sales skills for you and your workforce in any organization through regular practice and rehearsal to develop an understanding of the need to identify the customer's issues first in the initial meeting before moving forward. That first meeting is one of the most important steps to the sales process, and has fairly standard elements by any professional including:

1. Agenda Confirmation (emailed the day before a scheduled meeting confirming the appointment)
2. Go/ No-Go (or GNG) Criteria

3. Review of the Customer's Current Environment and Situation
4. Scripted Interview Questions
5. Clear Next Steps Component

The agenda is very straightforward and should just list the topics of discussion and clarify the reason for meeting. The tone of the agenda and the email sent the day before a scheduled first meeting should be very open to help clarify expectations of what the customer does and what both of you hope to accomplish.

A sample first meeting agenda in an email should look basically like this or at least have these components to it:

From:
To:
Subject: Agenda

Hello_____,

I am sending this agenda to confirm our meeting scheduled tomorrow at xx:xx a.m./p.m. until xx:xx a.m./p.m. Can you please reply and confirm?
First Meetings Should Include:
1. Introductions
2. Expectations
3. Your organization's current environment and situation overview
4. Overview of my organization
5. Possible solutions to work together
6. Current products/services or needs to quote
7. Recap/Next steps

Second Meetings would have the same email confirmation the day before the appointment and include everything above but replace "Introductions" with "Recap last meeting"

The Go/No Go (GNG) Criteria Component is right out of any military operating handbook of executing any plan. There are fundamental elements needed to execute on a particular operation, usually defined as the go/no go criteria, meaning that if the essential minimums aren't available to successfully execute on the plan, an abort criteria is established. In sales, that go no go criteria is established as the clarifying verbal vetting process to validate and qualify the person and opportunity to move forward at the outset of the first meeting. This verifies that your sales professional is meeting with the right person who can say yes to move forward. It's an opportunity for you or your sales professional to ask the customer to put some skin into the game and make a commitment if all elements needed to move forward are met, that they are at least willing to move forward. This is essential so no one wastes his or her time any further if there is no potential to go forward because there are others in the prospective customer's organization who may very well veto any decisions to switch suppliers put forward, or there are circumstances such as a contract commitment that can't be amended, or won't expire within a reasonable time frame to move forward with your organization. It is important that sales professionals balance their zeal to move forward with understanding the best use of their time. If the prospective customer tells you and/or your sales professional before this initial meeting even begins that they are not the decision maker on this contract for service, product or offering from your organization, your sales professional should hold off on moving forward to the next step of providing pricing or quotes. Also think twice about responding to bid requests until a fundamental understanding is reached about your capabilities and their needs and whether there is a fit in the future if not today due to timing. Your go forward criteria could be that you will present to another influencer or decision maker, but if so, you would want to set that expectation as an outcome of the initial meeting. Sometimes it the logical next step to the process of understanding needs and being able to offer solutions that fit everyone. At the very least have the customer understand what your specific go or no go forward criteria actually is so you do not waste time making fruitless presentations to people who have no input as to the outcome of the decision to choose your product or service.

Review of the customer's current environment should be an overview of how the customer is currently obtaining their products and services and should be the opportunity for the sales professional to ask scripted questions that identify opportunities to find matches in service or product offerings that can allow the two of your organizations to work together. With practice sales professionals really become experts in asking probing questions that would make Barbara Walters or the best investigative journalist proud. The point of this line of questioning is to get stories out of the customer and to draw out any negative emotions associated with past experiences. Sample scripted questions can be developed for a particular product or service that can help steer the conversation to uncover anecdotes that tie any opportunities to switch together for the customer:

- Can you tell me about your last or current vendor's product or service deliverable that was less than what you expected?
- Do you remember the specifics of what happened?
- How many times had that happened?
- What did they do to remedy?
- Did you have to ask them to remedy?
- Why do you think it didn't work like expected?
- How did this affect you?
- How much did it cost you?
- Have you any ideas on what you'd like to do next?

This line of scripted questions draws emotion into the discussion and associates the current situation as one that can possibly be improved upon, and helps the sales professional position the customer into the position of considering an alternative to the current situation (which is likely why they have allowed you in to meet with them in the first place). It is the sales professional's job to know when it is time to listen and let the customer decide on their own that it is time for them to try your organization out on the next opportunity when they need the product or service being offered.

In the overview of your organization's products and/or services in a solution sales environment, it is important that your sales professionals not delve into presentation mode too heavily, leave the customer with enough information to know that there might be a good fit, address everything that the customer needs and secure an opportunity to come back with a specific solution which would include a presentation of specific capabilities or products/services that address specifics in a more clear and holistic manner. Remember that your offering is probably similar or closely compatible with every other company's offering. The prospective customer is most interested in identifying the difference between you and everyone else in the first or subsequent appointments, and will want you or your sales professionals to get to the end of the presentation process as quickly as possible and show prices or your solutions so they can compare with the others and decide which provider is a better fit. It is imperative that your sales professionals not rush the process and allow themselves time to develop the absolutely perfect and customized proposal presentation that addresses every specific issue that was brought up by the customer in this first meeting.

It is best to leave the customer wanting more information and wanting your sales professionals to return with the customized solution, then to immediately receive pricing or deliverable solutions and rule you out without fully understanding the value proposition that you may have to offer. Depending on your products or services being offered, you could direct the conversation to attempt a trial close in this first meeting where you get an agreement that if your prices come within x% of what they currently are able to get the same products or services, will they consider moving forward with you. You will be able to identify right away where the prospective customer might be looking to fit your products or services in, or rule you out. At the very least you should be able to walk away from every meeting with some specific products or services that the customer has immediate needs that you can fill, even if they are simple communication deliverables to get back to the prospect within a set period of time so you can establish, maintain and build on a rapport and trust.

It is in that second appointment or meeting where the sales professional should continue the discussion and have prepared a specific presentation tailored to address the issues identified in the first meeting. This second or follow up appointments after the second appointments are where the rubber meets the road so to speak, because you should be able to definitely gain some kind of commitment from the customer to switch to your organization or to at least consider switching if continued milestones, expectations or parameters are successfully met.

It usually is a logical format to follow for the customer and sales professional. The key to the second appointment is to confirm that nothing has changed since the first visit. It is important to review details or quick highlights from the first meeting, the outcomes or deliverables met or answered to bring you to the second or subsequent point, and confirm there have been no significant changes since the first meeting and assumptions are the same. This process takes as long as it takes for first and second appointments and there is considerable work that goes into the second appointment to prepare the perfect solution from the details captured in the first meeting.

If your product or service is generic enough that it fits every possible prospective customer's environment and you only have one solution that fits all scenarios, then you can direct your sales professionals to close right in this first appointment, but generally speaking, a one size fits all approach isn't the best approach. The industry giants who have the same solution usually have the same approach and it is significantly better resourced and funded, and your advantage is really your ability to be nimble with a tailored custom approach with smaller commitment than the larger companies.

The hardest part of selling is very likely getting those initial appointments or developing business from scratch. Sales professionals usually know the basics of active listening to customers, mirroring and matching a customer's body language and tone in a meeting or over the phone, and are skilled communicators, but all of those skills can be developed and practiced as fundamental selling skills.

The most fundamental aspect of selling is following up. After qualifying a prospect send an email, letter or postcard thanking them for the opportunity to call them later. The idea of qualifying a prospect to schedule or book an appointment for a presentation is the goal. It is professional courtesy after any meeting to thank someone for spending their time with you or your sales professional. It is also customary and a minimum expectation to recap the meeting notes in a simple email with clear next steps identified from that meeting. If you are going to compete with the large industry giants, you and your sales professionals will need to be as professional or more professional in every aspect of communication with prospective customers. .

Measure Open Pipeline Results Frequently
After each initial appointment sales professionals must log the opportunity into some kind of tracking system. There are many standardized customer relationship management and sales force activity tracking systems on the market that can help you measure and track the effectiveness of individual professionals including Microsoft Excel products like Access or Excel which can be very simple tools, to more sophisticated developed cloud based platforms like saleforce.com. You will want to know and segment the various types of customers your team meets with or gets appointments and converts to sales, or know the reasons why you lost some bids or opportunities. Tracking data and measuring data is fundamental. You will be able to develop analytical patterns among department types, customer segments in similar industries, and you will be able to better direct sales efforts to the most effective gains. In every opportunity that is prepared and presented, you must assign some estimated dollar value to the opportunity initially. Those values can be adjusted later as more details come in about the opportunity and the quotes are refined, so you have a

specific understanding of prospective sales in your pipeline.   With this information understood by you and your sales professionals, you will know where you need to make adjustments either in the sales pitch, selling process, people selected to pitch or the prices of your products and/or services being offered.

Compare Sales Results Against Benchmarks
Whatever benchmarks you decide to put in place, you have to start at some measuring point as the baseline. A good place to start is your projected cash flow analysis and assignment of sales quotas to sales professionals as a budget requirement. Just be sure that when you have historical data points to benchmark against that you use those to establish ongoing benchmarks instead of arbitrary budgets that have no basis in history or the market reality, or else your budgets and quotas will not have much meaning to the sales professionals striving to achieve those results.

Adjust Sales Activity To Effect Pipeline Management To Drive Desired Sales Results
Once you have an understanding of how many calls, appointments, presentations, and quotes it takes to achieve budget, build in adjustments to improve on those expectations by putting in reasonable adjustments that are SMART (specific, measurable, achievable, realistic, and time-bound) pipeline goals. Generally speaking successful sales professionals are competitive and respond well to contests. Naturally those professionals who succeed in sales have internal goals as well as external goals, but consistently, most

successful sales professionals tends to appreciate a healthy and fun competition with their peers, with themselves over previous benchmarks, or other goals. Simple contests that give recognition have been effectively proven to drive results as well as contests with monetary value prizes. The impact on sales from contests has been legendary in organizations that deploy them for specific drives for fund raising, or increasing volumes of activities or sales. If you have a logical tracking system to measure the opportunity pipeline in real dollars and number of opportunities, you can begin to track the trends in sales performance to help you see that it may take an individual greater frequency of making more presentations to achieve a win than others or originally expected. You may have to make adjustments to your activities to get the sales results you want, but without understanding the elements going into the pipeline, you won't know where to make the adjustments..

Ideas To Action

Maybe you have good ideas about how to improve things where you work or live. Maybe you see opportunities for your employer or community to explore something new for the benefit of everyone that is not easily available to you, your employer, former employer or community. If you look around you may find there are ideas for new opportunities to solve problems all around that can be solved. You can get large industry suppliers or established industry players to sponsor solving the problem and helping you develop your idea for the betterment of everyone if you can convince them that there is a problem, a market of people who would pay for a solution and it is something that you can help solve. A great idea unexplored or tried by others may become the perfect fit for you to pursue as an entrepreneur or supplemental hobby or income. The idea behind an organization's existence should be purposeful whether for profit, non-profit, community, or individual family's unit. Whatever idea is the genesis of your organization's mission and purpose, it should be grounded in logic as well as passion. Entrepreneurial ventures that succeed are usually based on more than just the positive or negative cash positions possible and returns on investment of money or solely based on economics. Making more money is definitely a motivation. However if that's the only reason to establish a new business or organizational venture, then I would argue that an entrepreneur and the investors might want to reconsider a better use of their funds in an investment opportunity.

Good ideas have purposes behind them to make something better, add value to some current product, service or situation, or create something new that provides solutions to people, places or things that people didn't know existed before the new idea that came out. Who knew about a wireless device that could also allow the user to make calls, take pictures, surf the Internet, or play games or quickly accomplish tasks through custom applications? Ideas like Apple's iPhone product, or RIM's BlackBerry products spawned entire new industries of application developers and mobile marketing. They were innovative ideas that had some purpose behind them more so than the purpose of making money off the ideas.

Good ideas come in all varieties, shapes and sizes, generate positive cash flow and have a plan to get the right people on board to execute strategy and share the vision and passion of the idea. A great idea probably isn't going to thrive without the passion and drive of the enterprise's founders. A division vice president at a Fortune 500 company I worked at liked to use the expression: vision, passion and aspiration without execution is hallucination. He ran a $4 billion business division and was right about this point. The best ideas are not much without the execution to make it happen. The larger competitors in the industry you are in or entering have great ideas coming at them from multiple angles, and if they are great companies they listen to these ideas and develop plans to successfully execute on the ones they can with ample funding and resources available to them.

This section is about assessing your past experiences, educational background, and coupling the uniqueness that you have to offer to a new idea that you can envision solving. My goal in this section is to help you identify what would work for you and your particular customers. First assess your personal or organization's present situation. Ask what problems are left unsolved? Ask what problem or problems can't be solved yet and why not? Do an honest inventory of what resources and environment you have at this present time. Logically and critically think about current needs in the present environment for you, potential customers, the community or your employer. Visualize a potential future of what is possible by successfully executing on a plan of action around solutions to the present environment. This process should generate some ideas you can come up with to improve on anything in the present environment. Next, map out a list of tasks, resources and activities necessary to address what is keeping the present from actually improving to your envisioned potential future. The classic approach is to treat this exercise like a root cause analysis or "why" analysis asking "Why?" at every step. Ask "Why?" or "Why Not?" to the list of answers that come up regarding the tasks, activities and resources needed to execute on a plan to bridge the gap between the current or present situation to the future vision imagined.

By asking, "What don't we have? And asking "Why don't we have that?" as a follow up to the answers that come up, you start to see tangibly what needs to be overcome to bring the future vision to reality. Continue to ask "What has to be completed before the next task or activity?" and "What tasks or activities are independent of each other?" Do not to cloud the complexity of completing tasks or obtaining the resources necessary. This simplified project management approach to solving problems can be done collectively with a group of prospective customers, suppliers, larger industry players, trusted advisors, etc., that can help spawn new ideas to remain competitive, launch new projects or businesses or expand into new segments of customers.   By taking this approach your ideas are more likely to become tangible and real to you and you will have results that you can measure in terms of milestones passed along the way.

Assessing your past experiences and outcomes from trial and error and taking away the key learning points is the key to future success in the long run in almost any endeavor. One's ability to overcome, adapt, flex, and apply theory to practical applications and to improve on the day before is usually the secret ingredient that makes organizations and people great. Practical constraints or realities faced which can be barriers to executing on a great idea have to be minimized and overcome in order to pull off successful idea execution. Before you can even get to that point, you might have to recognize and address your own individual or collective bias based on your past experiences and education.

Many great ideas are not ready for implementation, because of timing or other factors in large companies, but those big companies have a lot of free cash flows to fund figuring out what they don't know and factoring what they do know into the decision making process based on critical thinking. In order to compete with these companies, you must do the same thing and figure out a way to differentiate and shows your organization's or your individual uniqueness that makes your idea competitive. It is easier said than done to find original and innovative products or service solutions that you can offer up as a competitive advantage. Apple continues to show the world what innovation is all about. The strategy of Apple's rivals seems to be to develop a product and/or service that is similar and as good as Apple's products, or better or differentiated by better price points, unique product or feature differences, greater or wider network availability.

As much as individuals and enterprises all have similarities we are also very unique. At some basic level we all know how to compete to some degree for resources and differentiate from one another. If you understand and accept the basic nature of competition and competition theory outlined with the five forces that affect an industry competing for business, then are you willing to subject your specific competitive advantage to objective scrutiny? Can you honestly assess whether you offer something that a segment of customers can deem competitively unique? Can you prove it with focus group research or studies? If you can't convince potential investors, prospective customers, suppliers or even family stakeholders to give you a shot at trying out your idea, you may yourself want to reconsider investing in your idea. When you prepare an idea for execution into a business plan that is going to be submitted for scrutinized review by potential customers, suppliers and investors, are you sure that you have been objective about the viability of your idea? What unique advantage are you offering the market based on your past experiences, expertise or collective education? Why do you want to execute on a particular idea? If you believe that your offering can stand up to the objective scrutiny assessment and evaluation based on your background, education, experiences, research, then you should be able to convince your collection of stakeholders including prospective customers, suppliers, and investors to help you get started. A clue that you might need to tweak your plan or focus on another idea would be if you cannot get enough agreement from objective backers including prospective customers, suppliers and/or investors to help you get started or keep you operating.   When a good idea is successfully executed, it will usually generate good results. Good ideas can be as simple as executing on delivering a slight variation on a very similar product or service as other competitors, but timing the introduction of the varied product or service in an effective manner before the rest of the field can catch up or adapt to the incursion. Smaller competitors can generally execute their speed to market on new innovative products or services faster than larger competitors, and should take advantage of the nimbleness of being smaller and more innovative.

The concept of making an entrepreneurial venture stand up to objective scrutiny is not to discourage anyone from pursuing their dreams of implementing a great idea and capitalizing on it, but to address the reality that most businesses fail in the first few years because the genesis of the idea itself was flawed. Original business ideas were never seriously founded in logic or critical evaluation of the idea itself, or objectively reviewed against the industry's five forces at work where that business was trying to compete. This happens in large and small enterprises all the time. The best example of critical assessment is a personal story regarding the best advice I received from a friend when I was let go from a company as a regional manager for my geographical inflexibility to move to the Midwest HQ when new management took over the organization. I was convinced, I had enough cash on hand and could generate positive cash flow and the essential knowledge to start a new sandwich making franchise, and a friend who was an investment banker talked me out of purchasing a franchise with my retirement savings by critically reviewing my reasons for wanting to start a business, and questioning what I really knew about running a sandwich shop from my background (other than my considerable experience in eating sandwiches). His critical questions helped me to see that I wasn't prepared for the kind of capital resources I would really need to get a venture like that off the ground, nor did I really have any passion for being a sandwich shop owner. I just wanted to be my own boss because I was angry that my former employer had forced me to quit or accept a drastic change by relocating to the company's headquarters.

An objective review and assessment of the idea of me owning and operating a sandwich shop proved to me that even though I probably could make a living owning and operating a franchised sandwich shop, I really didn't have the passion for it, nor did I really care about that business idea. I also came to the conclusion that the idea of me owning and operating a sandwich franchise was more based on the franchisor convincing me that I had enough capital to get started, and they would provide all of the necessary financing and training for me to be successful rather than me myself having to learn anything on my own about this business. I realized it was more the franchisor's idea and not mine, and they had little to lose with my investment and were structured in such a way that they couldn't really lose either way, and covered their losses very well.

I had a lot of willingness, and initially loved what I thought was my idea, enough to seriously consider doing it, and pulling retirement cash out and paying an unfavorable tax penalty for an early distribution, but really lacked the ability to be objective about the idea. Most of my family and friends were supportive of anything I wanted to do, and really knew that ultimately it was my decision, but my friend's objective questioning and critical reasoning with the focused approach of a potential investor was what convinced me that this franchise idea was probably not worth pursuing, and I moved onto a much more successful career.

Understand Your Present Market Condition

After you have objectively assessed that you have the right objective view and can apply your background of experiences, education and expertise to a given idea to actually start planning out the execution of that idea into a real business plan, your next step should be to really get a good understanding of the competitive landscape. Start the research on the industry and the five forces at work in the industry. Identify the biggest competitors or leaders, as well as major suppliers and the rivalry between the companies. Understand who the largest competitors sell their services to, and try to figure out why customers choose particular competitors. My advice is to invest a lot of time and energy understanding the customers in the market space and do your own original research in addition to paying for some professional research that is objective and not put out by the largest companies, but also talk to potential suppliers. Pay particular attention to different competitors' size, strategies and tactics. You should be able to answer questions about the industry. Is it an emerging new cottage industry forming around a new technology or innovation? Or is it a more mature industry potentially on the decline due to substitutes from new technologies or innovations, or fewer competitors due to consolidation? Is it hyper-competitive? Meaning that everyone is always undercutting the others with price wars competing for a shrinking pool of customers? Find out if the major suppliers have the capability and are integrating forward directly competing with their customers or if it is highly likely that it will soon be happening. Also find out if the largest customers and specifically a segment of targeted customers that you're interested in could be capable of building their own product or service offering internally and produce whatever it is that you would like to supply them by integrating backward into what you can offer? If so, you can develop a business plan to address any of these factors, but essentially do your own five force analysis. Make sure you know what kind of impact your idea will have on everyone in that industry. Exercise considerable energy and judgment to predict how that particular industry will react to the implementation of a new idea or way of doing business when and if you were to enter.

One pioneer in the office supply distribution business made an impact on the office supply distributor industry by being the first to offer a retail store for office supplies that served small businesses, and for the first time made standard price offerings for core office supply products that up to that point had been priced by contract stationers delivering directly to business customers from standard product line ups but varying gross margins set up for delivery. That office supply superstore and commercial distributor continued to innovate with new ideas in that industry by offering lower price differentiation, then free next day deliveries, then new offerings like copy and print services, facility janitorial and sanitation supplies. Their idea was to innovatively keep adding offerings that their same customers bought from other suppliers and create a sole source provider solution.

The example of the company above innovating into creating a one stop shopping experience for their customers caused reactions from the existing competitors in the office supply distribution business, but also a reaction from new competitors they didn't have before in the commercial print industry who saw the encroachment as a new entrant, and adjusted their offering by either lowering prices, adding new values to their services by offering more personalized or customer specific focus, or even countering by offering office supplies such as paper and toner to their customers. The industry leader in the paper and toner and office supplies business, obviously counted on a reaction by their superstore rivals and commercial office supply rivals, but they didn't count on the encroaching reaction from an entirely new industry of competitors of established commercial printers able to offer office supplies as commodity items to customers.

If you are going to compete with the industry giants and make your idea a reality then do your homework and know the strategies and tactics of the industry participants. Make an educated guess about the reaction of your new entry. Industry giants like the large office supply specialty retailer generate over $1 billion in free cash flow annually and may be willing and able to drop prices to buy market share and drive smaller less cash rich competitors out of the same space. Expect a reaction like this and have a cash flow model and contingency plan to address the price adjustment with a bundled offering additional value that differentiate your offering from the larger giant.

Once you have done a basic analysis on any idea that you have whether your goal is to make the proverbial mousetrap better, improve the efficiencies of widget making by an innovative design concept, create an innovative or funny script for call centers to talk to customers over the phone or whatever differentiation idea you develop, then you are ready to turn ideas into action.

You will need to anticipate multiple scenarios of reaction to any new idea for product or service in any industry. Will the larger competitors ignore the entry? Will they react by lowering prices; will they react in other ways like bundling additional services or strategically aligning with partnering businesses? Put together multiple scenarios grounded in logic and critical reasoning and model what you would do if the industry forces change. Make sure you have a contingency plan on how that could impact your new idea, and plan a contingency into overcoming, adapting and improvising to continue to compete. Go back to those business essentials that must be on a rock solid foundation in order to make your idea a reality. Make sure that under different pricing scenarios your cash flow still stays within an acceptable return on investment range for you and your investors. Make sure that if your customers defect that you have an acquisition and retention contingency plan to get them back or keep them from going in the first place. Make sure that you have multiple sources of capital reserved or credit facilities that can be potentially opened as part of contingency planning. You don't want to be in the middle of an order and find out that you need to obtain more capital in order to compete in a new environment. Also keep in mind that as your original plan regarding infrastructure needs could also change as result of entering into the market. You could easily require larger space, more vehicles, more employees, new product or service lines, new virtual capabilities in response to the competitors' reaction to your new entry. Put at least two alternative scenario models together to your cash flow, capital, customer retention and acquisition needs like an over and under for each original assumption to cover yourself. Can you scale up, or down? If your customer growth doesn't come as fast as expected, or comes way faster than expected, etc., My advice is spend time here in planning, and less time in reaction mode. Just pull the contingency plans down, and put them into play and continue to make adjustments.

If you still think the idea is a great idea after making two additional assumptions over and under your initial assumptions and you can live with the worst case scenario then it will prove to you to be a viable risk to go ahead with it. There are very simple cash flow analysis templates that you can draft up in MS Excel, as well as countless packages available on the Internet to help with business planning that can help you develop this plan.

An effective and inexpensive way to bounce a plan's viability is to contact local business school's outreach departments. You can also pay for advice from professional accounting and management consultants who specialize in your specific industry or are known for developing business plans in that industry. Also many major suppliers and even potential customer contacts like former customers or colleagues at former employers that you trust who are involved in the industry you intend to work in can provide a wealth of information and a different perspective. Their insight can prevent you from missing any unforeseen components or outcomes. One example of a potential miss averted for a supplier of warehouse racking systems, came from a relationship with a large commercial printer that warehoused and fulfilled print orders for one of their larger customers and used both typical racks and a unique automated bin system as an innovative space saving system that operated on rails more like a Laundromat system of hangers that came to the operator calling for an item by bin tag rather than a rack or conveyor system. In a rack system, the operators on a forklift or cart walked out to the rack and found their bin and retrieved the items for shipment which was a fairly standard warehousing solution, or similarly in a conveyor based system conveyor belts line a warehouse or cross dock facility to get items to their correct locations. The bin system concept was seen as an innovative solution by the printer's larger customer that when a new fulfillment center was being designed by the customer, the rack supplier to the printer who had learned of the bin system's innovation from the printer, was able to offer the printer's customer a completely new innovation replacing the typical rack or conveyor system and surpassing even the rail bin system with a newly invented autonomous wireless robotic bin system that traversed through the warehouse to the operators. This new innovation was originally inspired by the rail based bin system used by the printer, and the printer's customer and suppler both benefited from learning of the innovation from the printer and implementing a new solution.

There are many case studies that are published to advertise a particular business available online through Google in just about any industry topic. The marketing departments of companies make it a point to advertise their unique competitive offering that give a window into the particular industry that you are interested in researching. I highly recommend that you read all you can put out by the leading suppliers and customers in an industry you wish to offer services or products. I recommend reading as much as possible put out by the largest competitors in that industry as well. I also recommend that you do your own original research in addition to what the top industry giants put out as their marketing material, state of the industry and do not rely solely on other competitor's marketing materials and annual reports.

Execution and Implementation of Ideas
Once you have researched the competitors, suppliers, customers, and analyzed substitutions possible, and you have decided it makes sense to pursue the idea that

will allow you to compete in an industry, and you have analyzed the impact to cash flows, capital and infrastructure needed to execute, then it is time to execute on the idea. Execution on good ideas takes disciplined activities and leadership. The traits of leadership is where the rubber meets the road and where execution success meets reality. Many small and large organizations don't figure this out quickly enough and water down execution strategies with inadequate people who are little more than sycophants chasing quick investment opportunity dollars and happy to have project work for the immediate future. Many of these individuals can come from well-heeled, well-schooled, well-intentioned and even well-credentialed backgrounds but have at their core reason for involvement your idea the furthering some personal agenda. It could be to make a name for themselves and add the experience to their resume as a stepping stone to their ultimate agenda to do something else. Be aware of why someone wants to work in your organization and be sure to objectively separate genuine executives who will execute on the strategy needed with discipline and draw contrasts to identify those who are also qualified individuals and talk a great game, but are likely more interested in cashing in on an opportunity and will move on without concern to the next opportunity if the idea never gets off the ground, and have no personal stake in executing on the strategy required. Larger corporations often view executives as assets and hire individuals for very specific roles with the understanding that these assets can and will further the organization's agenda, and accept that these individuals also have their own personal agendas. One of the main advantages that a small proprietors or closely held corporation has over a larger public corporate entity, is that an equity stake in the success in the endeavor assures everyone that there is adequate skin in the game to execute to success with a disciplined and measured approach. If you hire like a larger competitor, and allow those executives to walk in and out of you venture at will, and possibly take your idea to a larger competitor, or worse compete with you on their own, you lose. Execution comes from having the right people on board. Anyone who doesn't have a real personal stake in the idea and may do a great job with the execution on the idea is not as committed to the success of the idea as much as you.

Execution on good ideas can become sloppy. The people brought into execute can operate in silos or with poor direction from leaders. If there is a general lack of understanding as to the reasons why the successful implementation of the idea is crucial to survival or worse the executives and employees don't really believe in the idea, but just work there, it is potentially disastrous for a small organization. If this is the case, leaders need to figure this out in order to execute properly and effectively and get the right people. It starts with the right people on the bus, and then getting them in the right seats on the bus, and then maintaining the right course to prevent the bus from driving off a cliff. The economic conditions of the last few years where unemployment is higher than it has ever been historically has led many employees, middle managers or senior executives afraid to voice their dissenting sentiments. Executives and employees asked to execute plans based on bad ideas or strategies that senior leaders have undertaken creates a secret understanding amongst the employees that the expectation in executing the daily, weekly, monthly, quarterly or yearly goals are unreasonable. In fact in many companies I worked for, the employees thought the senior leaders were actually stupid and knew that plans and expectations put in place would never work. The assumption was that no one in senior leadership would listen to any dissenting opinions. In fact in most large companies I worked in, dissention was viewed by senior leaders as insubordination or subversion of their execution plans. Leaders who were so far removed from executing on plans without adequately understanding the daily execution expectation were thought in need of having their heads examined for embarking on particular courses, yet no one would say anything, and just let dollars invested in project ideas literally fly out the door. A smaller more nimble company cannot afford to waste money on bad ideas, and has to recognize when it is time to change course swiftly. Circuit City Stores, Inc. is an example of leaders executing plans based on bad ideas that were conceived in a vacuum void of dissension from employees at the ground level. The leadership at Circuit City Stores decided that it would be possible to compete with Best Buy by eliminating their commissioned sales force and copying the Best Buy strategy of non-commissioned sales people working on their floors. They failed to listen to those commissioned salespeople who probably understood better than anyone the competitive advantages of Circuit City's differentiation through an incentivized sales force over Best Buy's model, which had always been a competitive advantage for Circuit City over Best Buy.

Modeling out possible outcomes is an important part of developing an execution plan. If in more than 35% of your potential scenarios, the outcome is less than your optimal or acceptable risk outcome, then it is probably too high a risk to pursue the plan behind your idea. Plans based on present conditions are probably easy to perceive as well as predict outcomes. But like with any activity, develop contingency plans in case the present conditions change and require different courses of actions. Try to predict how future outcomes could go. Make logical assumptions based on critical reasoning of courses of actions that you would take if sales, operations, or changes in the macro-economy deteriorate. Where and what will you cut first if you have to cut something out? Determine and plan up front what you are willing to put at risk, and when you are willing to cut your losses or vice versa willing to invest more into the venture to expand and capture more opportunity.

If you can accept the rule that you must take a risk to get some reward to get what you want out of life, the general rule of thumb is to minimize the risk wherever and whenever possible and optimize the reward potential outcomes at every turn, because it is not possible to predict the future. Educated guesses applying logic and critical reasoning can improve the possible outcomes to more favorable risk tolerance but in the end only you know how much risk you can tolerate. Only you know how much capital you can put at risk. Some outcome modeling may show that executing on a particular business plan will generate a much more positive result than you originally predicted. So build a business plan model with at least two additional outcomes no matter how likely or unlikely they may seem. When you weigh risks, rewards and calculate the multiple outcomes, you may see that the risk may not be worth the reward in executing on the particular plan to bring a new idea to fruition. Relatively and generally speaking with regard to risk reward outcomes, any idea which comes with logical business plans that model out with unfavorable risk-reward outcomes to your personal tolerance level more than 35% of the time probably ought to be scrapped. This means create a business plan with milestones of when you will break even and build in assumptions, then look at different scenarios and possible outcomes including delays in production of your product or service, or lack of sales within the specific timeframes as possible, and see what it does to your cash flow and capital position and see if the loss is too high for you and your investors.

Executing a business plan on the original idea you came up with goes back to your fundamental essentials, cash flow, capital, customers, and infrastructure as well as the time of when you will reach specific planned milestones. Model specifics of who, what, when, where, how and why in your business plan and plan to measure progress against milestones. When you have developed your plan and built in logical and most likely outcomes for your milestones, then model the alternative scenarios going over and under each milestone and identify specific go or no-go forward criteria. For example, you may plan that by the third month of operating, that you will have a certain number of customers ordering at a certain level, and provide yourself a contingency plan to step up activities in one or another area and either plan in to invest more or exit now and cut losses into your execution plan. This prepares you to change directions if required and actually gives you a framework of which direction to take at the critical time.

This is not a new concept to anyone, and there is no better example of executing on strategies and modeling various outcomes than the US military. There are contingency plans with redundancies built into almost every possible scenario that can be imagined by military planners addressing who will do what, when, where, how and why for events as far ranging as one country invading an allied country requiring the US military forces to assist, or to conduct operations to evacuate American citizens. Military contingency plans include scenarios as far reaching into the future that expeditionary forces could be pre-positioned in certain regions of the world prepared to conduct offensive operations against specific target or enemy forces or prepared with supplies, food and water to provide humanitarian relief anywhere in the world.

The US Marines go so far in their scenario planning as to pre-position fleets of ships with all of the necessary gear to logistically operate autonomously and continuously without need for resupply for over 90 days with the capability of putting a very large conventional war-fighting force (arguably more capable than the overall war-fighting capabilities of any other specialized or conventional military force in the modern world) on the ground anywhere in the world where there is access to a seaport within hours at the soonest and days at the latest upon receiving orders to execute on a particular strategy or order given by the president of the US.

At the personal level, most people plan for multiple scenarios to face the future. They answer what if questions in the event they lose a job or spouse's income tomorrow without warning or a sudden storm hits. They are wise to sock some money, water, fuel, batteries or food away in case of a power outage. Most people also figure out how much money and time they think it will take to find a new job, etc.   In business planning you would do the same thing, but to a much more detail level.

There are lots of great planning applications available like MS Excel or MS Project or other customizable business planning software applications and consultants that can help you design and logically create a business plan to execute on your idea. Just list out the fundamentals and start filling in the questions as to who will do what, when you anticipate it will be accomplished, what is interdependent on what else, how it will be done, and with what resources. The planning can get very complex or as simple as writing it down on a napkin at a restaurant as long as you are comfortable that you have the essentials identified and backed up.

Before thinking that you've put adequate time and resources into business planning understand that competing with industry giants and even smaller companies operating in the industry you want to enter have plans in place. The very large organizations have specific risk analysis criteria and also have developed detailed software or other internal tools to help decision makers implement and execute on new ideas. They have perfected business plan execution down to a science if they are an industry giant. If you don't take a similar approach you are at a disadvantage against them. They are well funded and rich in resource tools when it comes to executing ideas into a tactical plan of action. If you don't think you can keep up with that level of execution competence, then get someone on board you can trust, quickly who can help you develop your business plan.

Motivation

In order to execute a business plan on the next great idea you will need a disciplined approach and need to leverage your strengths. I highly recommend that you first evaluate your strengths and the strengths of the individuals you will be depending on to execute your business plan. I recommend a self-evaluation tool like Strengthsfinder 2.0[9] to help you evaluate your individual strengths and that of your prospective team members, as well as family supporters who you will rely on to execute on any business plan. You should complete and assess your strengths in the context of either this standardized evaluation format or some other format you recognize which can help you first identify your natural personality tendencies and help you understand the strengths profile of your colleagues. It is a foundation to developing a motivated team that will be able to work harmoniously and understand each other better. It has been proven to work wonders to create motivated, high performance teams because every member understands each other's inherent strengths and will be able to see ways to improve in areas that they are not as strong and possibly recognize ways to approach each other without as much conflict. In order to create high

---

[9] Strengthfinders 2.0 © 2007 Tom Rath published by Gallup Corporation and www.strengthsfinder.com are standardized personality profile analysis tests available to identify strengths in the context of individuals and interdependent teams. This bestselling book and test are a recognized standard for identifying personality traits.

performance, teams have to remain motivated and focused and keep a high level of discipline necessary to execute on plans. Whether that means tight cost controls, consistent selling activities, delivering outstanding consistent services or products that stand out from the competition or creating and maintaining an efficient business infrastructure that gives your organization a competitive advantage.

In addition to remaining highly motivated you will need to bring in employees, partners or suppliers who need to remain motivated at high levels giving 100% of their capacity to the effort of your organization. This means having people around your organization that are committed to the success of the overall mission or founding idea of your reason for existence. The teammates will energize others around the organization and passionately attract and retain customers, suppliers and investors. High performance work teams are assembled and remain at high levels of performance when the members are properly motivated to do their best.

Financial reward is one motivating factor for employees but not always the main driver to high performance. Employees derive motivation from inspiration to want to do better for their customers, employers, families and themselves. They will move in the direction of continuous improvement if they are challenged and motivated to do so. If financial reward was the sole factor, the 2010 NY Giants or Miami Dolphins should have represented the National Football League in the Super Bowl because they certainly had the highest payroll in 2010 at close to $140 million, yet they didn't even make the playoffs while other teams like the Kansas City Chiefs who only spent around $80 million actually did make the playoffs. High performance cannot be purchased outright without other factors put in place to inspire employees through words, actions and the opportunity to continuously improve.

If people are told how great they are doing, appreciated for showing up to work every day and thanked for doing their jobs in an organization, what message does that send them? That they are doing enough to keep the organization on track and maintain the status quo or meet the expectations set up for them. Essentially the organization is saying, we set these expectations up so we're not losing anything and you are working here every day to keep our organization in business by meeting the expectations of growth or performance goals set up for the position. The basic assumption by every customer is that the product or service they order from any source will be manufactured or performed to the specifications asked for and delivered on time. It is fundamental to why that customer trusts the organization with their order. So why are organizations at a loss when order volumes fall off or sales performance falls short of expectations in a manufacturing environment why would quality or deliverable output speeds vary? In sales it could be because of the macro-economic environment. More than likely however it is because an uninspired workforce has not adjusted to the macro-economic environment and failed to anticipate outcomes. The organization has failed to either create or enact their contingency plans on how to deal with the new market conditions. If the organization failed to plan for the new macro-economic conditions with a pre-positioned plan in place such as reducing prices or adding more value somewhere in the offering to meet the new reality to retain or add new customers, then they are already falling behind the original planned outcomes.

How does that happen? The leadership is asleep at the wheel. There are people in the organization uninspired by the business plan and are either not fully supportive of the plan and the changes necessary to improve and compete in a tougher environment or they are not seeing the need to change. How have leaders not been able to catch this? They won't admit the reality in many cases that they themselves created the sense of complacency through their own inability to inspire the workforce. They failed to demonstrate through actions and words that which will motivate and inspire the workforce to transform into a high performing organization that can withstand and overcome the headwinds of the new economic forces hitting their organization.

Inspired people volunteer to help themselves and others do better. They work longer, smarter and harder and do everything possible to improve things. When it is still not enough they ask questions as to what they are missing, what don't they know and what could be done differently to improve themselves and the overall organization. They challenge their status quo. People, when inspired, make all the difference between a high performing work force and a low performing one.

Leaders need to create this environment and figure out how to sustain it. Many human resource experts in organizations set up canned attempts to inspire employees with a one size fits all approach. For example, one employer I worked for had a numerical performance rating system of a numerical scale of 1 to 4 where it was considered unachievable to achieve a score of 4 and that a score of 2.5 out of 4 was considered meeting standards and a good score for an employee meeting expectations. A score of 1 usually was an indicator that the employee had some kind of deficiency and needed some kind of performance improvement plan or disciplinary plan. The performance appraisal score corresponded to the annual pay increase offered to the employees as a percentage of current pay. Employees understood that there was a connection to the score achieved and the merit increase given. Greater pay was possible for a better performance rating, but once employees understood that they could never achieve 4.0 out of 4.0, they stopped trying to do any more than the expectations of the job. This approach follows popular wisdom used throughout human resources managers and is the trend as the most efficient way to manage the performance of individuals in an organization. However this system completely fails to inspire employees to do more individually with this approach. One year when I threw the company's HR wisdom and scoring convention to the wind, and let individuals know that if they actually beat their specific performance goals, they would not only max out their numerical performance appraisal scores and achieve a 4.0 out of 4.0 on the specific performance appraisal category, but also improve the likelihood of actually achieving a 4.0 overall on their performance appraisals. Almost all of the employees on my team outperformed expectations and were able to beat their goals assigned trying to achieve a maximum score because they were inspired to achieve what was otherwise to that point unobtainable.

Every individual can be approached specifically and encouraged to do their individual best by their managers and leaders if the individuals' motivations are understood. Employers that take the time to understand their individual employee's motivations are far more likely to achieve high performance out of those individuals. If employers recognize average employee performance as good and regularly thank them for showing up and doing their jobs, they definitely have happier employees which logically would imply that their customers are more likely to be happy and stay loyal. Employers should never thank employees just for meeting expectations because it is exactly what it is implied, the minimum expectation. Since when does anyone thank anyone for simply existing? Any employee who falls below minimum expectations should immediately be addressed as to the problem and quickly removed if they are not meeting expectations or demonstrating the willingness or ability to meet minimum expectations. One large employer I worked for was so afraid of turning employees over but demanded such high performance that it was impossible for more than 50% of over 200 employees in a workgroup to meet the minimum expectations. The organization's leader's response to prevent turnover was to regularly thank individuals for the most menial accomplishments or meaningless achievements such as successfully making it through the day, week or month without hurting anyone or themselves. It was hard for employees to take the organization's leadership seriously about anything, because they never heard about how poorly they were actually doing.   The organization's leadership set a policy to publicly laud top performers for achieving goals while totally ignoring the underperformers. The effect of this continued policy allowed underperformers to remain on the company's payroll while secretly looking for employment with the company's competitors. Morale was so low within the organization that a culture of substandard performance was the norm to which others benchmarked, often remarking, that they shouldn't be fired or held accountable for their individual poor performance because others were doing far worse.

The aversion to turnover was intended to keep the organization safe from risk of harassment, wrongful termination or hostile environment lawsuits which became the driving priority to the organization rather than focusing on achieving high performance. This company tried as hard as they could to inspire better performance out of their employees but never was able to achieve even 75% of their goals.

As a leader assigned to this organization I recognized that the approach needed to change and negative performance as well as unrealistic goals needed to be addressed publicly and allow individuals to change to achieve their goals, or give them the opportunity to change their goals to be more realistic. As soon as I did this formally, the individuals who were unable to achieve even 25% of their goals were well over 75% and on their way to meeting their objectives. I took away any uncertainty that they felt and addressed high performance individually and publicly as well as poor performance individually and publicly to let everyone know there was nowhere to hide from poor performance and turnover while costly was not the greatest perceived cost to me, but rather underachieving on performance. The entire group's performance as measured as a group was over 100% to their original goals when they worked together as a team and understood that particular team-members faced challenges that would not allow them to achieve 100% of their goals, and so those that could over deliver on their performance goals, did so in the spirit of helping those who could not, so as an entire team they achieved 100% of their goals when measured as a unit. Peer pressure is an interesting and powerful motivator.

One of the best examples of a high performing workforce environment and how peers effect performance was learned early in my professional career going through the commissioned officer selection process at Marine Officer Candidate School in Quantico, VA. I had been a prior enlisted Marine where the average pace of running the physical fitness test (PFT) course of 3 miles was about 21 minutes for the average enlisted Marine. In fact a 20 to 21 minute 3 mile pace was considered pretty fast by most units running in formation. The minimum individual standard was to run 3 miles in 24 minutes and the maximum possible score was achieved by running 3 miles in 18 minutes. Having been enlisted for three years with various units where physical fitness was not a major priority for the unit's mission, I stood out amongst my peers in those units because I ran three miles individually at around an 18 minute pace. When I arrived at OCS, I expected to also stand out and lead the pack, but soon found that the whole class ran at a pace of around 18 minutes and that the leaders ran at a pace of around 17 minutes. After 12 weeks with these elite individuals, I learned that to stand out meant I had to figure out a way to run three miles in 16 or 17 minutes, and did, eventually.

The OCS instructors didn't have to tell me I needed to pick up my pace to stand out or address us as a group or individually as to where our performance stood. It was obvious from day one. I figured it out immediately after my first run with the group and it was abundantly clear to everyone there that this environment was different from any previous environments from where we came. This group was filled with highly capable individuals who came to a highly competitive OCS environment, and that graduating from this environment would take more than the minimum effort because the instructors would gleefully be proud to harass someone to quit and drop on request (or DOR) any chance they could weed out someone they thought was under-performing in that high performing and selective environment. Nearly 70% of the officer candidates that were accepted to the officer candidate course dropped out before completing the course and never became commissioned officers in the US Marines.

Bad organizations and leaders falsely create expectations which are either one size fits all or unrealistic to begin with. These organizations exploit people as part of their strategy to attract and retain employees for as long as they can for the duration of a particular project or until funding dries up. They operate human exploitation mills playing on a carrot and stick model of paying the minimum possible for performance to a high minimum unachievable objective. How would employees ever over-deliver on performance expectations in such an environment? Why would anyone ever want to take or show initiative in such an environment?

The culture of do more with less has come about from multiple efficiency gains, advancements in harnessing technology, process re-engineering efforts and systemic business improvements. Companies as result have cut positions and forced people to do multiple tasks and take on new responsibilities. Common sense has gone out the window. Doubling results with little more resources is not only expected, but happening at a huge toll on the very sanity of the employees left in organizations trying to manage the chaos. The general management rule of three or four direct reports to a particular leader or manager has given way to 12 or 15 direct reports to manage. One organization I worked for expected me to directly manage 53 direct reports and 6 indirect reports spread across five states. It is hard to inspire a workforce when they get little to no support from their leader who barely gets to spend the equivalent time of about one week per year with the individual. Flattened organizations that continually cut out their management resources are learning that they cannot support employees on the front lines.

Because companies run flatter than ever before people are seen as commoditized assets that can easily be replaced by others competing for the opening. These types of centralized control employers even pit the performance of one employee against others rather than create a collaborative environment where employees don't have to compete with each other but rather are encouraged to review and recommend their peers honestly for promotion to help choose their leaders. One well known proprietary chemical manufacturing company operating plants that produce raw materials used in everything from non-stick cookware to automotive parts created a new plant and experimented with making the entire plant entirely self-directed with no specific centralized controlled management structure. Every employee was an equal peer and equal stakeholder in the success of the plant's operations, product output, and employees rotated into new roles of the plant's operations, sales and management every 6 to 12 months. The results were this plant was one of the most productive and successful plants in the company using a peer based review system and an environment of collaboration which in turn led to higher performance in the overall plant which served as a model to the other plants in the company's portfolio of manufacturing lines. The experiment was a direct shot across the bow to negotiate better or more favorable terms with organized labor operating the other plants in the portfolio, telling them to improve relations with management or look at the alternative of domestic plant closing or restructured non-unionized workforces in the future.

Employers who set up unrealistic expectations face high turnover usually equal or higher to the percentage of employees not meeting the employer's minimum expectations. If the turnover percentage or if the percentage of employees not meeting minimum expectations is above a natural 15% - 20% (which is due to advancement or natural events not related to performance), then it is not a high performing work environment.

The situational leadership model well known everywhere in business schools and management circles in American business outlined in the One Minute Manager[10] and the situational leadership model known as the Hersey-Blanchard Situational Leadership Model taught in every business school's leadership curriculum in the US since 1972[11] has held up to be a universal truth of effective leadership and is probably the best approach to manage individuals based on their readiness levels to accept tasks assigned by a leader. For example the model becomes very clear in that a

---

[10] One Minute Manager © 1981, 1982 by Kenneth H. Blanchard and published by Blanchard Family Partnership and Candle Communications.

[11] Management of Organizational Behavior © 1972 Paul Hersey and Kenneth H. Blanchard and published by New Jersey Prentice Hall.

new employee hired into an organization has very high willingness to do anything, but may not have the abilities yet because he or she is new. The leader assigning tasks to this individual must be more direct and give clear and specific directions to help this employee complete the task, no matter how simple. For example a brand new employee eager to demonstrate his willingness to be a team player who has been hired to analyze widget making may be more than willing to take out the evening's trash. However, being new, the boss may have to tell him or her that the bundle of trash must be tied this way or that way, put in this or that particular bin facing in a particular direction because experience has shown that if it is not done accordingly it doesn't get picked up the next morning or that evening by cleaning crews. In the same example if the manager tells another employee who has been there for many years and is a trusted team player who has demonstrated both high ability and high willingness to accomplish any task to take out the trash the manager would not need to give specific directions or really have to coach or sell the idea of the importance of getting the trash out because the experienced employee has done it many times before, understands why it needs to be done and can simply do the task when it is delegated to him or her. If the manager gives specific direction or sells the importance of completing the task to this employee, it could that employee to wonder why his manager thinks he or she needs such specific attention to detail when delegating the task and either causing unnecessary friction or confusion between the two.

Following the same example to a third employee who is not brand new to the organization but still high in willingness to get the trash out for the manager, but not quite sure exactly how or why it needs to be done specifically the way the manager originally showed him or told him when he or she was brand new. The manager would take a different approach to coach this individual to help clarify the abilities needed to get the job done. In a fourth scenario where an employee who has been with the company a little longer, and has taken the trash out every night for the last week may know full well how to get it done and his high on ability to the task, but is low on willingness because he has to catch a train or something right after work and doesn't think he has time to get it done the way it needs to be done and thus has lower willingness but full well has the ability to accomplish the task. The manager would approach this individual differently with a more selling than coaching approach of why it's important to get the task done on time correctly. In the case of the trash not being bundled correctly or the bin faced correctly could cause problems, and the manager would approach the conversation in a different manner.

This base model of Situational Leadership is the foundation to achieving any high performing work environment because it requires the leaders to understand their individual contributors personally. It is hard to do that with 53 direct reports in five states and only 52 weeks in a year. The situational leadership model sets up the foundation for communication related to tasks, but only goes that far. In order to inspire employees to high performance it takes the traits and traits of good leaders practically demonstrating for followers the traits of JJDIDIEBUCKLE (judgment, justice, decisiveness, initiative, dependability, integrity, enthusiasm, bearing, unselfishness, courage, knowledge, loyalty and endurance) and not just charisma or speeches to evoke inspired and sustained high performance. Good leaders demonstrate effectiveness through actions and positive communication and motivate employees by inspiring those employees to go beyond their current willingness and competency levels. Inspired employees go out and enroll in evening classes or spend inordinate amounts of personal time figuring out ways to improve their own work performance and their organization for their customers and themselves. These employees gain a great deal of satisfaction and fulfillment from doing so, and also maintain a balanced life with family and community.

How many employees do you know volunteer for additional work or enroll in learning new subjects in collegiate or vocational classes at their own expense in order to not only improve themselves, but also to improve the organization they work for? What inspires them to do so? Maybe it is just the realization that they need to learn new skills in a changing environment, but maybe there is someone who inspired them to take on the challenge and believe that they can improve everything around them. Great leaders inspire people in a way that allow people to think their improvement efforts and choices they made were entirely their own ideas. If the leader puts a premium value on continuous improvement at the foundation of everything they do, it tends to inspire people to do more and achieve high performance.

How does an average organization create leaders that can develop a deep connection at personal and professional levels with people? It starts with the leaders themselves having a vested interest in every person associated with the organization. How do large companies spread out all over the world compete with that? CEOs and executives in large industry giants attend leadership and motivation training to help them develop the skills necessary to try to develop these personal and professional connections with their people, but only the sincere can pull it off. A small competitor who values his team like a family puts a premium on his people that no large company can match, and when you educate the small competitor with the leadership values that they need to develop like large great organizations utilizing JJDIDITIEBUCKLE and walking the talk every day, employees in that smaller company are more likely to accept greater challenges for less costs than the larger industry giants. Most employees working for industry giants are working there because of the pay and benefits as the primary reason and motivation for coming to work every day. It is actually a bonus in a large industry giant to also have leaders who put value on listening to individuals as well and thanking individuals for great results and encouraging an environment of professional creativity. It is rare in large organizations that they can accomplish this. I have yet to see it done in multiple industries and large enterprises. I have only seen it in enterprises where there is a direct connection with the owners or senior leaders.

Sometimes building the best team means displacing people to let them find their perfect opportunity and fit on another team or company they believe in. It is important to be consistent about it though. Once a decision is made on someone being a fit on the team, don't hesitate to act quickly. Definitely never settle on hiring someone who does not perfectly fit your organization when making hiring decisions. The Marines running officer candidate school quickly remove officer candidates that don't want to be there and never let someone with a negative attitude or subpar performance hang around too long to influence the other motivated members of the class that want to accomplish the next task and graduate. The Marines act quickly and decide early in their indoctrination and evaluation processes who will fit in the organization. The instructors are charged with making evaluative educated judgment calls based on early impressions as to who will successfully graduate. They instinctively know who needs to go and move quickly to apply pressure on those that are not a good fit to drop on request and quite literally make it known to those individuals that they don't think there is a good fit and step up the harassment.

Business life is not the same environment where you can harass people to quit, but rather there are employment guidelines of fairness and equal opportunity that are appropriate to follow. There is never a reason to discriminate against someone based on any perceived non-fit based on race, gender, religion, etc., that are clearly ethically wrong, but also clearly illegal in most of the United States. However, it is your organization, and if you find someone is not a good fit, or is no longer a good fit for the direction the organization is going, then you owe it to yourself and that individual to let them know as soon as possible that you are going to go in a different direction without them, and sincerely try to help them get along with dignity to their next position with another company or organization, and you owe it to them and yourself to do everything possible to make their transition smooth and easy. It says a lot about your organization and you as an individual. Organizations and individuals that don't understand or practice treating people with dignity pay a karmic toll 10 fold over time.

Consistent actions by competent, caring leaders who challenge employees to improve on their own abilities create environments where mistakes and failures are seen as opportunities to learn and improve. Those opportunities create a safe environment for the right people to achieve high performance. A safe environment for employees to learn from their mistakes may seem like a costly and risky type of business model, but it is inevitable that even the best and brightest people brought into any organization will make mistakes. It is absolutely essential to their development that they learn from those mistakes and improve themselves and the overall organization. Every high performance work force is made up of individual contributors who are individually inspired as well as share connections with each other and get inspiration from their peers and leaders. Individuals who repeatedly make the same mistakes in a high performing environment may not be in the right role, or they are the wrong person for the organization. There could also often be some outside factor affecting their performance which happens to anyone. In an environment with open and honest communication and dialogue between leaders and employees, a high performing workgroup will not accept failure and repeated mistakes and will find ways to help each other win as a team and win with consistency. Employees need to be free to do their best and leaders sometimes need to get out of the way of those individuals who need the freedom to be great. Individual contributors should be allowed to pour as much passion that they can into something they believe in because it usually will lead to great results. Consistency from leaders who allow mistakes must demonstrate consistent communications and actions that proves to everyone that there is consistent consequences to individuals that make mistakes. Leaders cannot be seen as inconsistent. For example a leader who hammers an individual they don't personally like for an honest or simple mistake while forgiving another individual who they personally favor or like creates an inconsistent environment for the leader, and the entire organization can see the inconsistency. Some individuals may think they get very far in their professional lives by sucking up to their bosses or clients and generally live their entire professional lives in denial of their true feelings about their jobs, clients, bosses, organizations. I am sure you know individuals who feel privately one way about their peers, organization or leaders but never voice their true feelings because doing so risks revealing their true feelings.   I couldn't disagree more and could not live or encourage anyone to live in such an environment of fear or illusion. The only person they harm is themselves and their families that they support by staying in such an organization and living a professional life which is basically a lie to themselves.

The greatest impediment to high performance is accepting average performance. In order to infuse high performance, leaders and managers at all levels have to be free to allow subordinates to think on their own and over-deliver on expectations, and encourage them to do so and accept that there could be disagreements between leaders and followers.   If there is a healthy environment where leaders actually listen to their people, there is actually the possibility that those employees could be right and foresee something that the leaders never anticipated. There are contributors including customers and suppliers who can enhance the original ideas and make the overall differentiation between other competitors in the market even greater. Encourage employees in a high performing work environment to get more education on subject matter that can be relative to the customers they work with. If you can afford to pay for their education, make the investment a gift or added benefit of joining the organization. No greater gift can be given to high performing employees than the opportunity to improve their knowledge which in turns benefits your customers, your organization and the employee.

Managers who don't understand consistency often discuss fairness as being the same thing. Consistency is more valuable to motivation than fairness. If all employees are consistently communicated with in the same manner, held to the same standards of high performance and consistently challenged to improve their individual contributions, and in turn celebrated when they over-deliver on expectations, then they become motivated and inspired to do better even when they are doing their level best. Perceptions on fairness are never equal. What is fair to one employee may not be perceived fair to another. It is important for leaders to distinguish consistency with fairness.

Consistency is also a double edged sword. If leaders are consistently non-communicative about what's happening, consistently negative in their collective and individual messages or set unattainable standards of performance that don't allow employees to achieve positive results then that team will experience declining morale and performance. The team will never reach its potential of high performance.

High performers have many of the same leadership traits and principles as the organization's leaders and founders, and those traits should be highlighted, encouraged, celebrated and looked for when recruiting. There is no room in high performing teams for blowing smoke at people, or an organizational lack of integrity in setting unreasonable expectations on people. The high performers in an organization like to be around other high performers and usually want assignments that demand high performance. Motivate these high performers by challenging them consistently, acting in a manner worthy of leading them through any initiative, demonstrating loyalty, earning their trust and in return expect high performance and their best beyond what they thought they could do individually and collectively as a group.

Staying Relevant

No matter what idea that is generated to create a new product or service or enhance an existing offering for development, at the core of all ideas should be some relevant value to be added into the market space. Warren Buffet has epitomized the concept of staying relevant to his organization, the many organizations he touches through Berkshire Hathaway as well as to the entire business world at the current age of 81. His uncanny ability to understand the value of a business, the leaders of that business and the long term relevance or staying power of that business in the industry in which it competes is what created the wealth of his Berkshire Hathaway holding company.[12] Buffet is so influential that his advice, counsel and wisdom are quoted in the US presidential election campaigns as a voice of reason to get the economy back on track and get Americans unemployment back to manageable levels. The man remains relevant despite never having worked in any job except the jobs he created for himself because he understood value better than anyone else and quantified it in such a way that amassed huge gains in capital.

The key to staying relevant is in the secret of Warren Buffet's ability to see the value of something before

---

[12] The Snowball ©2008 by Alice Schroeder and published by Bantam Dell is the official biography released by Warren Buffet in 2008 when it was speculated that he was retiring.

others see it and to capitalize on the advantage that can be gained by either strengthening that value for long term growth or whatever objective you want to gain. The fluid nature of the forces affecting all industries are similar and only competitors that can create or add real value can remain relevant over the long term. This value comes in all shapes and sizes of businesses from family diners that remain in business for multiple generations serving a specific niche community to large enterprises that hold innovative patents, unique intellectual property and can create monopolies on their proprietary products or services. Everyone and anyone can compete and find a niche that makes their particular offering unique in the way they offer a product or service. Large enterprises can differentiate and create value through better buying power and pricing or bringing economy of scale to bear for customers. Smaller enterprises may offer value by bringing faster speed of implementation to market. Individual proprietors who come up with unique technology or new patents can add or create value by introducing their new product or service offering. Building a better widget or proverbial mouse trap with better price points to the existing competition is fine for a time, but to remain relevant the value that was initially created or added to the product or service will eventually fade with the expiration of patents unless you figure out a way to sustain that value over the long term and remain relevant.

An example of how pharmaceutical companies remain relevant is by introducing a new drug to the market which is unique and patented for a period of time.

When the patent is set to expire and multiple generic brands emerge to contract with manufacturing plants to release their generic lines, the original pharmaceuticals make efforts to buy up all the potential manufacturing capacity in the world by releasing their own generic brands either directly or through subsidiary companies before their competitors can get to market. It may seem anti-competitive and even unethical, but it is an effective strategy that keeps large pharmaceutical companies relevant.

In order to remain relevant a business has to be prepared to invest in innovative solutions to new challenges that come along. For example, a local Chinese restaurant may be well known for their particular Chinese food in the community. However they may one day discover that younger patrons find it easier to choose restaurants through their mobile phone applications that call out menu specials along with directions, menu, available tables and expected current wait times, and allow the patrons to make reservations right through the phone. The restaurant may not see the need to make an investment in advertising or creating smart phone applications, but as younger patrons who could easily be interested in dining at the local Chinese restaurant choose other places to dine, guided through their smart phones, they will not remain relevant in a changing environment where smart phones guide individual dining choices, and may eventually go out of business if they don't keep up.

Understanding the value propositions offered to the end user and the latent problems in delivering products and solutions to the end users is an essential element to remaining relevant. It is an ongoing commitment to understanding the market you are competing in. The sooner your unique value proposed solutions become implemented into executable actions, the sooner industry forces will make adjustments to the new innovation and the unique value proposition you came up with becomes less unique. So how do you stay relevant? What is your relevancy plan to adjust when the forces of your industry adjust?

Relevancy can mean just about anything to anyone. For example, one organization may introduce a new product and understand that others will duplicate the product offering, but that being first to offer the unique product for as long as it is economically viable is their competitive advantage and they challenge themselves to come up with another product that they can introduce first. 3M is a good example of a company that introduced flat roll adhesive tape products and continued introducing flat product offerings introducing post-it notes and continued to introduce products like flat air filters for home heating and air conditioning systems. If the organization is already dominant in their industry such as Wal-Mart in the retail industry, their relevancy could easily come from expanding into new areas offering services directly to commercial customers in the business to business solutions space like banking or financial services or in offering their own brands of manufactured products.

Relevancy means planning the obsolescence stage of any product or service offered and   remaining focused on customers and competitors to keep up with demands or trends for new offerings. For example, obsolescence is planned into components on everything from refrigerators and cars to software and phones. There was once a time when it made sense to buy a refrigerator once in a lifetime for a household every 30 years. The components that made up the refrigerator were engineered and built to last 30 years. Service was readily easy to come by and it was much cheaper to fix a refrigerator if something broke down than to replace the refrigerator. The relevancy plan by refrigerator manufacturers was to keep selling new models every seven to ten years, and so they engineered refrigerators with components expected to fail expected after seven to ten years of normal use and parts costing as much as half of the price of purchasing a new refrigerator. This keeps the refrigerator manufacturers relevant over the long term. What is especially interesting is that manufacturers often deem parts and support no longer available or offered for older models to perpetually keep the customer in the market for a new product every seven to ten years, and by innovating with new bells and whistles to the standard refrigerator offering so that customers will want the newer models versus paying to repair older models. Microsoft is very good at staying relevant in much the same way. Just try to get support for older versions of Windows from Microsoft or any other hardware or software provider that discontinues an older product to force customers to upgrade.

One of the best ways to stay relevant is to develop a mechanism that allows you to listen directly to your customers. Make regular and frequent visits to the customer and try to understand your customer's base of operations by asking questions as if you were a new employee there.   Ask questions like who, what, when, where, why and how such as "who are your customers?" 'What do they do with your product or services?" "When are your sales at peaks or low points cycles?" "Where are your customers? "Why do you do something this way?" and "how do your customers respond to changes?" Staying relevant requires that you understand not only who your customer is and their organizational mission but asking how do you help them accomplish their mission. You need to understand this as much as you need to understand your own organization's mission.

You can gauge your customer's products or services offering to their customers by putting yourself in the shoes of their customers or end users of the products or services being offered and use focus groups and surveys of the end user community to best understand where your customer is positioned in their market space. Can you help your customer better understand their position in the industry or spot a trend that can help them stay relevant, such as the example of the Chinese restaurant and the smart phone applications? Can you introduce them to solutions that solve problems?

Introducing solutions to problems that the customer didn't know about and proactively identifying potential solutions helps you and your customer stay ahead of the competing forces of the industry. You attract and retain your customer who in turn attract and retain their customers and you both continue to offer a relevant and steady stream of products and services as solutions that you have created. The idea of creating or adding value to any relationship is a cornerstone to relevancy. GE is a worldwide household brand known as an American conglomerate multinational company that provides everything from light bulbs and airplane engines to equipment lease financing and insurance to small and medium size businesses. When they find that their American customers' orders are on the decline and that their customers located elsewhere in the world are on the rise, they adjust and scale down manufacturing in the US (ending jobs in the US essentially and contributing to the unemployment in the US) and scale up in those countries where the customers are located creating a booming economy for countries like Brazil, China and India where they make investments. To proactively maintain relevancy in their home country of the US, their CEO joins the Obama administration as a jobs czar. The Obama administration actively and publicly makes clear that they are investing in companies that make green technologies. GE secures their position as a relevant company by producing alternative power generation technologies providing solutions that will not only attract US governmental support and investment, but supposedly also create jobs in the US to contribute to the economic growth of the US economy. You can't be more relevant or apparent than GE providing value to the US government and securing their long term future in this country and the world as a corporate leader.

Staying relevant and adding value comes from insight, education, experience, and making good investments for future growth. You may find that your customers are forced to merge with competitors to stay relevant in their industry which is common. Consolidation in industries is something you can almost count on. Do you find that more than 25% of your revenues are coming from one customer? Or that 80% of your total revenues are coming from just 10% or 20% of all your customers? Then you are in dire need of new customers. You may find that a whole new competitor emerges from an acquisition or merger if your top customers merge with an entity not familiar with your product or service offering. What is your contingency plan if that happens? If you don't have one or can't imagine that it could happen in the near future, I would tell you to plan for it now. Start working on a plan to target and replace your top customers with new relationships and constantly work to develop multiple relationships through multiple customers in a particular segment, all of whom have the potential to grow your revenues to the point of never becoming larger than 25% of your total revenues. This may seem like a ridiculous thing to say if your products or services can only be sold to one entity like the US Federal Government, for example, because the innovative product or service you make or offer is of a highly restricted or proprietary technological nature applied to defense or intelligence assets used by the US Federal Government. However, the same rule applies to these providers of products or service sold exclusively to the National Security apparatus or the

Department of Defense. How will they stay relevant if the Federal Government decides to cut funding or changes priorities about funding? One way would be to develop applications for those exclusive products or services to be offered to the commercial market place. Potential solutions include securing business information or analytics, or applying commercial uses for military projects. If you are a small entrepreneurial minded employee of one of these large corporate giants, or an employee in the government sector and can envision a solution that bridges applications to commercial use, then you are well on your way to competing with the industry giants by helping those industry giants as either a customer or value added reseller, or as a supplier providing particular expertise or insight as a service provider to the industry giant looking to enter a new market.

It is hard to argue that research and development efforts take considerable investment. One might also think that it is hardly a business essential to invest in continual research and development because it adds to your immediate overhead costs with no foreseeable or immediate return on investment. I would argue that you must include R&D investments right up there as part of an essential business element that deserves to be backed up like the circuits on your manual transfer switch like cash flow, customers, capital resources, and infrastructure if you can afford something toward it. The question you have to ask is can you really afford not to set aside something for research and development? It may not be an absolute essential in the first year of a new organization's life to continue operating because considerable R&D probably went into launching the organization into existence, however to remain relevant after the second or third years, many new business organizations fail to plan accordingly or invest enough into R&D that will keep them in business beyond their initial introduction phase. These businesses bump along competing in the market space with the industry giants gaining more ground over them, and year after year they defend their market position as best they can. To some organizations it is enough to stay relevant by staying small and true to their core values and customers remain loyal to them, while the majority of small businesses actually get squeezed out of the market because they can't differentiate, compete or address changing customer needs.

The ability to stay relevant means an openness to change tactics or alter a strategy that you assumed was your organization's current opportunity of focus for the immediate future and immediate focus for your current investments. To remain relevant you have to have an open mind and recognize when your plans need to change and be flexible enough to change course and adapt and overcome the changes to your industry and your offering. If you can keep your focus on the end users of the products and/or services that you offer, you are in a much better position to remain relevant and innovative by adding new products and services that will continue to add value to your customers. Your offerings, while available from a crowded field of competitors, can still stand out because of the innovative approach you take in delivering your products or services that includes focusing on improving the deliverables of product or service to the end users or your customer's customer. This sets your organization apart, and opens new channels of business opportunities over time.

You may one day also find that remaining relevant sometimes means actually merging or strategically aligning yourself or your core offerings with someone else that when merged or aligned strategically the combined entity makes a larger impact on the market space and can better compete with the industry's giants. A great example of relevancy for an industry is the very mature and hyper-competitive commercial print, copy and promotional products industry made up of many thousands of fragmented participants who if united together own the largest share of the market (approximately 80%) while 20% is held by a few hundred participants. The print industry has seen forward integration from traditional customers like Staples, Office Max and Office Depot going from being relatively small resellers of print services to acquiring and strategically aligning themselves with very large commercial print and apparel manufacturing capabilities themselves to become very large industry giants with increased buying power and influence over customers and suppliers. These big box office supply retailers enter the print industry fairly easily overcoming the entry barriers of capital, infrastructure, cash flow and customers needed to succeed and innovate by offering their existing customers of office supplies a unique position of a one stop shop for both office supplies and commercial print from one convenient source.

In turn, smart commercial printers introduce common office products that customers would need like paper and toner as well as software solutions or other related technology services to counter the incursion from the big box retailers into their space. Most traditional commercial printers, who have been in business for generations, wouldn't imagine carrying an excess inventory of paper or toner or any supply items in inventory to offer their customers because their core competency is seen internally as producing print or manufacturing specialty promotional products. The physical space that they have available is dedicated to manufacturing and temporary storage of raw materials required to manufacture print or promotional products. Those printers that either merge or align themselves with the big box stores or other wholesale office supply distribution channels maintain an open mind and make it convenient for their customers to order from one source like the big box retailers and remain relevant and are in a better position to hold their position against the incursion by the big box retailers.

Priorities

Only you can set the priorities for yourself and your organization if you are the founder, leader, or in charge of any endeavor. If you leave a successful career to retire or resign before retirement, or your career ends abruptly, you may look to venture out on your own. Once you figure out what motivates you and gives your life purpose and meaning (outside of the career you just left), you will need to set up your priorities for tomorrow and the day after that, and the days after that. If you decide to set up a new enterprise or organization and know what your priorities are going to be, then you have to live by your priorities. Most people prioritize themselves first, their families and relationships with friends next and work or someone else's priorities last.

If your priorities were to create a company or organization that is going to achieve great things and you will seek fulfillment working toward achieving those great things then your priorities will probably be defined by those accomplishments and creating the action plan and milestones to achieve those accomplishments. Your priorities could also be that you wish to remain independent and earn a simple living wage or you wish to join an organization that pays a wage that you can accept and allows you the independence or ability to achieve the great unique contributions you can offer their organization to be fulfilled.

Priority planning is important for your health and the organization you create or work within. You can't have everything equally weighted as a top priority. While individual priorities are what you will measure against milestones every day or every week, for the purpose of setting up an organizational business structure with consistent priorities that line up with the essentials that you defined, you can set your priorities around those fundamental essentials of cash flow, customers, capital and infrastructure. If you find yourself and your employees focused on activities that aren't directly related to those four essentials, then you probably ought to reconsider the priorities of tasks you or your organization is focused on.

If you decide to go out on your own and do your homework on the interests and venture you want to enter, and you have an understanding of the business essentials needed including pricing strategy, capital, cash flow and sales volumes required as well as the customer base you must target and the activities necessary to achieve the sales required to stay in business and in positive cash flow as well as employees you will need to recruit and retain, then you probably need to start prioritizing tasks and setting goals. Your priorities have to remain in check and you have to review the priorities periodically.

Essential Priorities In Order of Importance to A Business Organization

1. Cash Flow - you have to measure sales to track that you have enough cash flows coming in, and adjust any conflicting priorities or activities that you're working on to maintain a healthy level of cash flow that holds up to your cash flow plan. This really means that you have to focus on sales and have enough coming in to cover your cash flow plan, and if not, then focus on your sales efforts to achieve your budgeted plans if you want everything else to fall in line.

2. Customers – just as you would measure your sales and track your cash flows against your plan, you need to develop a customer satisfaction and acquisition metric that prioritizes customer satisfaction and new customer growth as a priority right behind cash flows. Customers should be the main driving reason for your organization's existence because without them you wouldn't need to produce something or provide a service. Many customer tracking metrics for relationship management are available and effective. It is up to you to understand how important this essential strategy actually is and to continually check how you are doing with customers against what you expected for a given period. Set SMART goals that can be measured and reprioritize other daily distractions that will come up to make sure that at any given moment of whatever it is you or your organization's people are doing, that it is positively effecting the customer. If it isn't being done for the purpose of attracting or retaining

customers, you have to question why it is a priority.

3. Infrastructure – This essential priority has to be attended to as well as the other top two, but is probably less an essential priority to have to worry about unless it is indirectly supporting the other top two priorities. For example, you can't make your customer's deadline without a new piece of equipment, or raw material or collect on the order for payment without efficient enough systems that allow you to focus on the top two priorities. If you have an ecommerce offering, store front, warehouse or manufacturing infrastructure, it needs attention. The infrastructure can't be neglected to the point that it hinders the other more important priorities. If you find your attention and your organization's attention is spent on developing infrastructure like operations and missing the higher prioritized milestones originally planned like sales then you have to look very hard at your priorities. You may need to adjust your priorities to get back to the basics of why your organization exists and what your personal goals originally were. Are your current activities so focused on improving operations infrastructure taking your eye off the ball and causing you to miss your original organizational or personal goals? It is very common among new entrepreneurs to invest too much time in operations and infrastructure continual improvement and not enough in customer

service and the primary cash flow priority of ongoing sales.

4. Capital – you should also not have to worry about measuring access to capital until you come across the need for more of it, which is only a matter of time if you are growing at a fast pace. It remains an essential priority for any organization. Positive cash flows and effective customer strategies can alleviate some need for continually grasping for more capital for acquisition of assets or opportunities. As a priority capital is an essential that you need to keep an eye out for continued access to capital sources through banks, stakeholders and investors, but it is less a focus than the immediate needs of positive cash flows and customer retention, because without these two you don't really have a great need for more capital.

If you can align these four essential priorities up with your daily activities and measure with consistent frequency every week or every month, and you and your employees can end each day saying to yourselves that you in all earnest did everything you could do for that day toward the priorities that you had for that day, and they were aligned with these essentials, then you are well on your way to establishing a successful endeavor that will last and will be able to compete with the industry giants for a business venture. You may have a non-profit organizational venture or belong to a government agency or operate within a much larger enterprise undertaking a new enterprise or acting on a new idea or plan. Priority management is an essential to high performance people and organizations. Keep at the core of your organizational value system and you will be able to compete with the industry giants.

Priority Conflicts
It is only inevitable that every day there will be distractions and personal priorities that pull you and your employees away from your organization's core priorities. It would be unreasonable and unrealistic to look at priorities in any other way and it is essential that your entire organization understands your priorities when they and you get pulled away from them. Know it is going to happen and plan for a way to get back to your core priorities. Don't let yourself or anyone get caught in the tall weeds trying to figure a way out. Plan for priority conflicts and have a recovery plan for your organization.
A very simple measure of the right people in the right roles in any organization focused on the right activities is to have them all evaluate their individual priorities and rank them. Anyone who has used a Franklin-Covey planner or attended a time management seminar or uses Microsoft Outlook knows about the alpha-numeric ranking of priorities into 3 levels of urgency or importance using a quadrant model created by Stephen Covey to help people understand what their individual priorities really are. Most people prioritize family relationships highest, then personal friendships and work relationships and set up tasks and activities around these priorities. If the school calls you and tells you that your child is sick and needs to be picked up,

most people will drop what they are working on and either go pick up their child, or if they are not in a position to do so will spend the next several moments figuring out a solution to take care of their family situation first and then get back to whatever they were working on.

Many facilitators teaching time management open up their discussion holding an empty large jar and tell people to fit golf balls, marbles, and then sand into the jar. They demonstrate that the jar represents the priorities of life the golf balls being the largest ones represent family relationships, the marbles (or the second largest items to be put in the jar) as the personal and work relationships people hold dear, then the fine sand all the smaller priorities that they encounter during the day. The demonstration shows that if you fill the jar with the fine sand (representing work priorities) there is no room for the other priorities in your life (represented by the marbles and golf balls). Likewise if you fill the jar with all marbles, there is no room for the golf balls (representing family); however there is still room for the fine sand (or work related priorities). The demonstration goes on to show that if you fill the jar with all golf balls (or family) there is always some room to fit a few marbles (friendships) in as well as fine sand (work related priorities). Usually the demonstration ends with pouring a bottle of beer into a full jar of golf balls, marbles and fine sand to demonstrate what you prioritize there is always room for beer.

Educating employees or family member to recognize their individual priorities and put daily activities into perspective and ranking their list of priorities is important to individual and organizational development. This allows them to plan to accomplish in a given day all those things that need to fit in the jar, and maybe change the paradigm or perspective of the employee or family member to prioritize the company as the golf balls and put them in first prioritize them equally, and consider the rest of the stuff in their lives as the fine sand that will always be able to get done if their values and the organization's values are aligned.

I am suggesting that employees and their families balance work and life together to be congruent priorities and not mutually exclusive to each other. I am not suggesting employees take their work home with them and live their work without balance. Your employees and family must understand that individuals can prioritize family and work together and still maintain a balanced existence. Individual family priorities encroach into employee's productive daily tasks and activities and can sap the productivity in any organization if those individual priorities can't be balanced with the organization's priorities. Let employees plan for it with contingency plans to deal with emergencies and others who can cover for employees without losing productivity.
One effective technique to help employees and individual maintain a healthy balance of priorities in their daily activity planning and goal or milestone achievement is to use a simple test before embarking on any particular activity or task that is going to take more than a few minutes of an employee's focus. The 4 way test used by Rotary International members to

determine if they should get involved in something is a good model for priority planning. Rotary members ask themselves before jumping into something: Is it the truth? Is it fair to all concerned? Will it build goodwill and better friendships? Will it be beneficial to all concerned? This simple 4 way test that Rotarians use to build a better world is as good a model as any for building a daily activity and task priority list applying it against individual priorities balanced with the organization's priorities.

You and your employees first have to communicate and publish the organization's priorities in such a way that it is at the top of their mind when conflicting priorities present themselves. The essentials of organizational priorities should start with whatever your essentials are but should at a minimum include the basic 4 essentials your business or organization needs to compete with the industry giants. Simple questions employees can ask themselves as a 4-way test before undertaking tasks and activities are:
1. Is this going to improve our positive cash flow?
2. Will it better establish or improve relationships with our customers?
3. Will it control costs or improve our capital?
4. Will it benefit the organization's infrastructure?
If the activity can't pass this simple four way test it probably shouldn't be a priority activity or task.

Priority planning and activities need structure and using a structured approach to your day and week allows you to measure actual performance or accomplishments against that structure. If you do all your activities and priorities in your head and don't need a plan, structure, calendar, watch, smartphone or other device which tells you when to meet with someone or call someone, or remind you of future events you have scheduled then you are probably not in an organization that needs a priority plan because there are enough conflicting priorities to require planning. Most people however in 2011 need to use something to track, manage and remind them of events and activities. My advice is use all of the great tools that are available and the sooner you get multiple people in your organization on one calendar of events and some kind of organizational activity plan, the sooner your organization will be competing with the industry giants in the most effective way.

So assuming you plan your priorities in a recorded format and try to stick to your prioritized activities every day or every week, how often do you check yourself against your priorities? Once a week? Once a day? Once a month? Once or twice a year? It's up to the individual. The point is, in order to have a priority plan you have to check yourself and your organization's progress against the original plan. You can't measure success any other way than with time bound goals and milestones that you set out to accomplish.

Organizational Spirituality

Does an organization have a spirit or soul like an individual? One employer I worked for touted that their company had a soul which included things like being a diversity employer and being a green company and demonstrating ethical principles and espousing ethical values among employees. However their words hardly matched their deeds or actions of senior leaders. If they really believed their organization had a soul, I think many employees would have considered the organization's soul as dark as night with an evil menace at its core because it was sued multiple times and settled with employees on multiple occasions including class action labor abuse issues as well as orchestrating generally unfair and illegal non-competitive labor agreements with employees that were akin to legal terrorism forcing employees into accepting unfavorable terms for fair competition or dispute. Depending on your philosophy, many organizations adopt the same values that their founders believed in when they founded their organization. Does a for-profit on-going organization have an obligation to care about their employees or community in which they operate or where their employees live? Does an organization have an obligation beyond the legal regulations mandated upon organizations to pay a minimum wage to employees or provide safe working conditions? Does an organization have a duty beyond regulation to not pollute the environment or promote green initiatives? Does an organization have a duty to stand up to discourage and help eradicate the exploitation of children in the world? Does an organization have an obligation to set maximum working hours and allow time off for employees that protect them beyond legal mandates? If you believe an organization collectively made up of individuals working together in harmony and spirit can be greater than the sum of the individuals then I would say you also agree that an organization can have "spirituality" which is connected and bound by the beliefs of the individuals who make up the organization.

In order to compete with the industry giants an organization of any size has to understand and define its own set of values that are aligned with the individuals who make up the organization. In order to compete effectively, they must also then convey, communicate and portray those values collectively as an organization to demonstrate to the market what those values actually are. It could be as simple as employees volunteering to hand out water at a local 5k or 10k charity race or actually sponsoring a charity with cash donations. Whatever the level of commitment and capabilities of the individuals who believe in helping their communities, the organization collectively should encourage and promote this activity and most importantly communicate their involvement.

Industry giants have giant coffers from which to fund charitable events and organizations to generate goodwill in their communities, and although smaller organizations can't compete dollar for dollar in donations they can compete by demonstrating a greater percentage of their giving in real dollars compared to the industry giants. In terms of real organizational contributions, many communities would not be surprised that large industry giants won't give up one tenth of one percent of their total revenues as a giving strategy. A much smaller organization is often willing to give as much as ten percent or more of total revenues to try to match donations by larger organizations and garner goodwill in the communities they serve. The revenues in small organizations are so much lower that the impact of employee volunteering and putting dollar value to their contribution is a tangible and measurable comparison that any community can make objectively as to which organizations are more aligned with their values and deserving of support by the community.

Corporate giving is good for business. Large organizations with lots of cash to use for giving know that they can exploit the goodwill of a community or patrons from giving small tokens relative to their overall revenues, but large dollars to any community. Exxon Mobil is one of the largest companies in the world by revenues with 2010 revenues reported of approximately $383 billion, and earnings of over $30 billion, while they gave a whopping $237 million worldwide in 2010 or .06% of their total revenues. Yet this corporate giving of $237 million buys serious goodwill to allow Exxon Mobil to capture resources all over the world despite it not necessarily being in a particular local community's long term best interests. One only need look at organized religious organizations to understand the size of the goodwill that can be gained and the transformative power of a large constituency that can be influenced to make purchasing and/or voting decisions based on the goodwill generated. So why not be a force for positive attributes to the community and generate goodness where possible regardless of organized religious beliefs or ties. Most if not all religions are based on principles of virtue and goodness at their core and are largely universal in their base of demonstrating kindness to others, general goodness to all, honesty and harmlessness to others.

The universal law of karma which is what goes around comes around is a universal law as much as gravity is a universal law and is the foundation of many religious philosophies of the world. Organizations that understand, embrace and work within these universal laws are better positioned to compete in the long term and those that skirt these laws end up short of greatness. All major industry competitors to some extent have adopted some corporate or organizational philosophy or belief system grounded in good behavior toward employees and customers, fairness to their employees and customers beyond just the minimum mandated regulations and laws and try to communicate this to the communities within which they operate. There is no mandate or regulation that says organizations must give something to a charity, promote diverse work environments and create aggressive and measurable models of fairness for employees in their organizations. However the largest source of tangible donations to charities comes from organizations collectively made up of individuals volunteering or donating to their favorite charities.

Individuals that make up organizations fundamentally understand their spiritual beliefs are sacred and inherently their individual choice. Organizations like corporations are not mandated to give anything but those who do benefit.

The sooner your organization adopts and understand this concept and differentiates from the others with regard to having an organizational spirituality plan that ties individuals to the collective organization's values, the sooner that your organization will be able to compete with those larger companies competing in your industry. Give what your organization can to the community then look at what your customers do and what they give to in their communities, and to the next level, their customers in turn, until you get directly to the end users in the customer chain. Then look at what's important to those end users based on their demographic peculiarities. See if you can translate your employee's giving or volunteering to some of those specific groups to generate the goodwill around your organization that larger industry competitors often can garner and exploit.

Your organization can effectively give a higher percent to total revenues per specific event or donation drive than larger competitors because their revenues are so much larger and even though their total dollars generated for giving may dwarf your organization's giving with the charity, make sure your constituents, stakeholders, and customers supporting the charities understand the percent to total revenues that your organization is giving. Don't be afraid to draw comparisons to the larger industry competitors to see who can make a more impactful contribution. Let the community that you serve what their endorsement to your enterprise could mean to them if they can help your organization grow its revenues because you are clearly more willing to give a larger percentage of your total gross revenues or earnings. If your constituent community understands this concept then they are more likely to help your organization grow revenues and endorse your business or even provide referrals for a measurable volume of increased revenues from giving. All you have to do is acknowledge and actually share with other the facts about your organization's collective good work made up of the good work of the individuals in your organization.

Organizational spirituality goes way beyond delivering a product or service that provides some value or benefit to customers, and delivering it at the price agreed, and in the time frame expected, as well as honoring returns fairly and consistently or owning up to mistakes quickly. It is also understood that providing a level of customer service that is personal, effective and grounded in customer centricity is a basic for any organization. A basic fundamental of organizational spiritual diversity includes treating employees with respect, consistency and valuing their diversity. Diversity values that favor or endorse subpar performance in favor of political correctness to some specific ethnic or minority interest group is wrong and does not value diversity, it is political pandering and should never be tolerated because it undermines true organizational diversity where equal opportunity for quality high performers are given a chance based on capabilities and performance. Also basic fundamentals require an organization to address the sustainability of the world and making the world a better place for all inhabitants which means not contributing to pollution in favor of short cuts to improve cash flows. These are universal givens for any successful organization. If you can't build these basics into the organization's philosophies of selling a product or service, and address these basics, then you should question why you are in an endeavor to compete in a market space with others who see these organizational fundamentals as basic elements that need to be innovatively improved on to compete. It also doesn't ever excuse bad behavior. If larger industry competitors treat people unfairly, compete unfairly by taking shortcuts to improve cash-flows blindly, pollute the environment or otherwise violate the universal laws of nature karma will take care of the organization and your spiritually guided organization will prevail over time.

Organizational spirituality takes all of the basic tenets of all of the individuals in your organization's beliefs into account, brings them to the collective table and values them to the point that your organization basically puts out what would be the equivalent of a pot luck luncheon spread of opportunities for the entire organization to join in one or all of the giving opportunities presented. To arbitrarily decide that everyone in an organization has the choice of one favorite charity or organization near and dear to the leader's heart is not only going against the universal law of karma, but is very bad for the untapped opportunities that exist from understanding and valuing the diversity of your organization's individuals. See giving for what it is an opportunity for you or your individuals to contribute and do some good for the world and benefit from the good work.

Universal Truths, Rules & Essentials of Life

So much material is available on the fundamentals of life that it is impossible to adequately summarize the greatest philosophical works published by the organized religions, and the philosophers that formed the framework of societies and governments. However today in business there is a vacuum of what I'll simply call essentials of good conduct, fair trade and the recognition of universal truths, rules and essentials of life in modern business that must be obeyed in order to compete with the industry giants.

For the purpose of wrapping up this discussion on how to compete with the giants in industry and applying some universal essentials I've observed in business in the US and to some extent the world over. I have compiled them into the following general rules or truths that hold merit worth considering for you:

1. <u>Survive to thrive</u> – you can't thrive if you are struggling just to survive day to day, week to week, month to month, quarter to quarter, year over year – unsure of the unknowns and ill equipped to face them head on. Get the help you need to get out of the survival mode you might think you are in, face your fear of unknowns with action plans, a realistic strategy addressing the fundamentals you need, and visualize what you will need to accomplish to

thrive. It is the first step to abundance and thriving in a truly fulfilled way.

2. <u>Right to compete</u> - in the market space. Large industry barriers and forces of an industry would have individuals believe that the forces which create monopolies or oligopolies for products or services are too difficult to overcome. However just as Thomas Jefferson in writing the US Declaration of Independence declared: "We hold these truths to be self-evident, that all men are created equal, that they are endowed by their Creator with certain unalienable Rights, that among these are Life, Liberty and the pursuit of Happiness," I would argue that everyone and any organization in any country has the fundamental capacity to compete, survive and thrive in doing what brings them fulfillment.

3. <u>Corporate structures are overrated and unnecessary to compete</u>. Good organizations can compete without the limiting liability protections of a corporate structure if they don't engage in activities that cause the risk to reward balance to be overloaded to one side or another, and can accept individual accountability to shareholders and owners. The advantage that corporations share is to limit the liability of their shareholder owners to attract more capital for use by the corporation allowing anonymous shareholders to trade shares openly in a public market place or privately through closely held

corporations. It is unnecessary if an organization can raise enough capital through its internal efforts and through the support of its own constituency including customers and owners who stand by their product and service without limiting liability. As a customer wouldn't you prefer to buy a product or service from an organization that is completely accountable to you if they cause you harm or damage due to negligence, mistakes, omissions, errors or greed? Would industries such as finance, utilities, insurance, banking, tobacco, oil, healthcare, pharmaceuticals be the size, scale and so willing to take risks if all the shareholders that owned those companies had unlimited liability for the damage that those companies could be held accountable for? Would malfeasance or misbehavior even be possible if investors could personally be held accountable for blindly allowing their owned operations to take excessive risk? No way! You can compete openly and add unique value and raise capital completely on your own if you have stakeholders like customers, suppliers, partners, family and friends who believe in your organization's capabilities, and you compete fairly and in an ethical manner.

4. The best defense is not to offend. There are inevitably going to be disputes between competitors, suppliers, customers, but they can be eliminated if you follow the advice of this rule. Wronged parties will always seek remedy

for perceived offenses. Everything under the sun can be argued through due process of legal proceeding or binding arbitration which is consistently applied through free and fair society, but the fact remains, it costs everyone and society something. If you can avoid disputes altogether by engaging in practices that don't offend or create the impression of wrong, and can resolve disputes quickly and quietly before they reach the point that a third party must mediate or arbitrate, then you and society win in the long run. The key is to understand the frivolous nature of litigation and the calculus that must go into engaging in disputes. At the very least set a minimum threshold for an acceptable loss before engaging in the frivolity of a lawsuit in a dispute (whatever percentage of your gross revenues as you see fit to accept). If it costs you zero to defend or to bring forth a claim as a plaintiff then consider the opportunity cost to reputation, energy, distraction from what you could and/or should be doing that is core to your mission. You'll probably realize soon enough that whatever the outcome of a dispute, it is not in anyone's interest to waste time, resources or capital in litigation.

5. <u>Life is a long journey with very few straight lines.</u> It is not always possible to see around the curve or bend in the road ahead or beyond the horizon, and so if you know that you can't see around the corner but embrace the journey anyway you can find a niche in which to

compete. Knowing this, you just have to get up every day and take action and do what you were put on this planet to do and bring your uniqueness every day. Whether you work for an industry giant, small competitor, or are out there on your own, bring your level best every day and plan for the future but keep your planning flexible enough to adapt and overcome to whatever comes around the corner.

6. Pick battles carefully. It is inevitable that on your own or in any organization you will be competing more than collaborating and partnering with others who do not share your views, enthusiasm, vision, or passion. Or you will come across formidable competitors, some who even leave the rules of ethical conduct at the door, and compete in ways that you couldn't or wouldn't. Always remember what battles are worth waging and go into these battles with your eyes open and completely focused on your objectives. Understand that engaging in any battle you will have to accept the worst outcomes possible and move on. It could mean having to walk away and finding another way to make a living. However if you believe in your heart the battle should still be waged then fight to win. Act decisively and move quickly to bring as much strength as possible to bear on the weakest component of your opponent's defense. It is never acceptable to not fight for what you believe is right and necessary to fight even if you are not sure you will win; In fact it is as much a

universal law that it is your duty to fight to win, as much as it is your duty to honor your commitments. If you lose so be it, you still must fight without concern for loss because you have picked the battle carefully and are only fighting because you have to. Consider the entry fee into battle so high that you hopefully never have to put all of your enterprise's very existence at risk, but if you have to, you must do so without concern for losing it all. Go into it with the understanding that it is already forfeit before you engage in the battle. Small battles with a co-worker, boss, spouse, customer, competitor in the market, etc., really become ridiculous when you submit this entrance fee to fight this battle. Understand that the opponent may also have made a similar commitment and carefully make the distinction to only fight the battles that need to be fought. If you approach every battle this way you won't engage in battles just to prove yourself right or just because you think you can easily win. You would and should only engage in battles because you fundamentally need to win to continue existing.

7. <u>Honor commitments and build trusting relationships everywhere.</u> If you can accept that there are leadership traits and traits to strive to develop, maintain and surround yourself with then you should be able to grasp this fundamental concept that trusting relationships are the foundation of successful and happy existence for organizations as well as

individuals. The minimum expectation with anyone is that you will do what you say you will do, mean what you say and write, and strive to forge trust between everyone you and your organization come into contact with. To forge trust means you have to be somewhat transparent in your dealings, be honest and straightforward without hidden agendas, undue secrecy or trying to gain unfair advantage over anyone or anything. It also means not exploiting anyone or anything just because you think you can get away with it or no one would ever find out. Many industry giants have fallen down and lost major contracts, deals or reputation because of violating trust. Don't be tempted by the potential gain that can come from shortcuts or skirting around trust. If you can't be fair, open and honest in negotiations up front and you find the need to resort to confusing specifics, details or fine print that allows you to change pricing, add additional charges or modify terms or conditions to an agreement with the other party, something might be wrong. If the other party doesn't fully understand something at the onset of negotiating agreements you could have trust issues that come up later. By and large, if and when the other party does find out that you did not adequately disclose something up front or explain it well enough for them to understand something you will lose trust and it is very hard to recover trust.

Conclusions

The keys to competing with the industry giants comes down to self-confidence and trusting yourself enough to know that you have what it takes to pull it off as an individual leader. You possess some or all of the JJDIDTIEBUCKLE traits and can build on those leadership traits over time and strengthen your position as a leader. Acknowledge where you come up short and recruit for employees or suppliers that have those traits you need to provide customers a more competitive advantage.

Understand your essentials to whatever it is that you're going to attempt to sell from cash flow to the specific customer segment that you can carve out, and how you will approach them, and at what price point you will need to set up your operation. Understand the importance of cash flow, and capital resources and always improve on the infrastructure of your operation to improve on the customer's experience and make it easy for the customer to do business with you. Make sure you understand that the essentials to your business have to be backed up with redundancy in case something happens to your primary means of operating. You need to be prepared way beyond disaster recovery preparedness of flashlights and extension cords but essentials backed up in the circuit panel where you can switch to alternate generation resources. You need to set your operation up where you can flip a virtual switch to keep everything running smoothly. This helps to be better prepared for transition whether employees quit, die, or you are forced to fire them. Customers may defect or lose funding for their products or services they were buying from you. Emergency cash expenditures will come up that deplete your cash reserves or outstanding opportunities will arise out of nowhere and require you to tap capital assets banks or borrow money from anywhere and everywhere to stay afloat or capitalize on the opportunity of your lifetime. It is going to happen at some point. Plan for it, and know that you can address it when it happens.

Focus on selling. Hire the right people for selling your brand, products, and services. Don't settle for less than the ideal candidate. No matter how challenging the operations, don't take your eye off the focus of honing your selling skills and your entire team's selling skills including the operations operators. You never know when a customer will come through for a tour or will need someone to make a personal delivery. Keep them ready at all times for a customer facing experience. Motivate yourself and your people often! Don't let employees or yourself get lost in the weeds or off track to what is your core mission or purpose for existing as an organization. Thank people often for doing great work and going beyond minimum expectations.

Don't stop looking for ideas to improve on something or innovate in some way for an existing or new customer. Always check yourself against your competition and remain current and relevant to your industry. Never stop looking for answers as to how to help your customer's customer or end users. Write out your priorities, and don't let yourself or others get too distracted or away from those priorities that you measure against on a regular basis.

Remember to always infuse your strengths, your beliefs and that of your team into the community and customer base you serve. Help out the charities that you can, encourage your family and employees to help out and give time or whatever you can give, and make sure your customers and the community know that you give and care. Lastly live by the essential rules that will get you through anything, and you will never have any regrets about anything you do, and you will compete so well with the industry giants, that you may end up becoming one or partnering with one.

www.ingramcontent.com/pod-product-compliance
Lightning Source LLC
LaVergne TN
LVHW051635080426
835511LV00016B/2341